Thomistic Triumph

Overcoming Obstacles to Enlightenment

by

Dr. ant

Contents

Suggestions for Further Reading

Suggestions for Further Reading

Chapter 1: Thomistic Triumph: Overcoming Obstacles to Enlightenment

In the annals of history, few have soared to the intellectual heights attained by Thomas Aquinas, a beacon of erudition and a tower of spiritual fortitude. Verily, his journey was fraught with divers obstacles, each surmounted with the grace and tenacity that hallmarked his quest for enlightenment. Let us embark upon this narration, chronicling the trials that beset our hero and the triumphs that heralded his ascent.

Thomas, born to the noble Aquino family, was from the outset destined for greatness, albeit not without traversing the vexing valleys of adversity. The era into which he was thrust was replete with scholastic rivalry, doctrinal discord, and societal upheaval. It was a time when the intellect was both sword and shield, and Thomas wielded these with unparalleled skill.

The first of the many barriers that stood in his way was none other than his lineage. Nobility, though a blessing, was also a bane, for his family envisioned a future for him that strayed far from the cloistered life of contemplation he sought. Yet, Thomas, in steadfast piety, saw his calling not amidst the pomp and pageantry of secular power but within the hallowed halls of the Dominican Order.

Resolute in his aspirations, Thomas encountered resistance from those dearest to him. His family, vexed at his choice, endeavored to sway his resolve, entrapping him in a year-long captivity within the familial castle's confines. It was within these confines, however, that Thomas's spirit, rather than wither, flourished. Herein lies his first triumph: the dominion of faith over filial piety, a testament to his unwavering commitment to God's calling.

Upon his release and subsequent entry into the Dominican Order, Thomas embarked on his scholastic voyage, a journey beset with intellectual rigors. His insatiable quest for knowledge propelled him into the heart of Paris, the then-epicenter of theological and philosophical inquiry. It was here that the next formidable obstacle emerged: the skepticism of his peers and mentors.

In an age where intellect was currency, Thomas's unassuming demeanor masked a mind of unparalleled depth and breadth. His contemporaries, quick to judge by outward appearances, initially underestimated his acumen. Yet, as his ideas began to circulate, the tides of opinion turned. The once-dismissive voices now clamored for his insights.

Thomas's triumph over skepticism was not merely personal but emblematic of a larger victory for faith and reason. He challenged the prevailing notions of his time, advocating for a harmonious coexistence between faith and rational inquiry. This was a radical departure from the dichotomy that had long existed, setting the stage for what would become the cornerstone of his legacy.

Yet, the path was fraught with further tribulations. The very novelty of his ideas drew ire and accusation, branding him a heretic in the eyes of some. Here, Thomas faced perhaps his gravest challenge: defending the orthodoxy of his beliefs against the very institution to which he had devoted his life.

Armed with nothing but the shield of his convictions and the sword of his intellect, Thomas entered the fray. His defense was not merely a rebuttal but a profound testament to the depth of his faith and the breadth of his understanding. In the annals of ecclesiastical discourse, few moments shine as brightly as Thomas's vindication, a resounding affirmation of his doctrinal soundness.

Even in health, Thomas's journey was not unburdened. The rigors of his scholarly pursuits took their toll, rendering his body frail but never his spirit. It was in this physical vulnerability that Thomas's strength of will shone brightest, his pen never ceasing, his mind never waning until the very end.

The crowning triumph of Thomas Aquinas, however, was not in the accolades he accumulated nor the volumes he penned but in the illumination of the path towards enlightenment. His lifework stands as a beacon to those who navigate the murky waters of doubt and disbelief, guiding them towards the shores of understanding and faith.

In our present age, where skepticism abounds and faith oftentimes wanes, the legacy of Thomas Aquinas beckons. It is a legacy that transcends mere scholarship, embodying the triumphant union of faith and reason, the very pillars upon which he built his life and works.

Thus, the tale of Thomistic Triumph is not merely one of overcoming obstacles but a narrative that kindles the flame of inquiry and devotion within us all. It is a clarion call to embrace our own quests for enlightenment, fortified by the lessons of his life—a summons to traverse the path laid by Thomas Aquinas, guided by the light of reason and the warmth of faith.

In the chapters that follow, we shall delve deeper into the life and works of this colossus of Christian thought. We shall explore the essence of Thomistic theology, the trials and tribulations he endured, and the indelible mark he left upon the tapestry of faith and reason. Let us proceed, then, with hearts open and minds attuned, to glean from his wisdom and partake in the triumph of Thomistic philosophy.

For in the journey of Thomas Aquinas, we find not only the map to intellectual and spiritual enlightenment but also the mirror reflecting our own pilgrimage towards understanding and belief. It is a journey fraught with challenges, yes, but illuminated by the perpetual light of truth, guiding us ever onwards to our divine calling.

Introduction

In the annals of history, where the luminary minds of theology and philosophy etch their indelible marks, stands a figure both venerable and formidable—Thomas Aquinas. His life, a testament to the pursuit of divine truth, beacons those ensconced in doubt and unbelief towards the light of faith. This narrative endeavors not merely to chronicle the journey of this great saint but to argue, with vigor and conviction, that Aquinas's intellectual odyssey is a beacon for the modern soul adrift in the sea of skepticism.

Forsooth, in an epoch where the shadows of atheism and agnosticism spread their gloom, the story of Aquinas shines as a luminary of divine reason. It was he who, in the midst of medieval darkness, sought not the extinguishment of questioning but its baptism. With the lamp of logic and the oil of faith, he endeavored to prove that Jesus is indeed the incarnate God.

The sagacity of Aquinas, a jewel among the intellects, signifies more than mere human genius. It serves as a bridge between the ethereal realm of faith and the concrete domain of reason. This work posits that it is not through ignorance but through understanding, not by blinding oneself but by seeking, that one comes to know the divine.

Engage, therefore, in these pages, with minds open and hearts attuned, for herein lies not only a story of a man but an invitation to traverse beyond the mundane, towards the sublime. Aquinas's life and works, an epitome of the quest for knowledge subordinate to faith, challenge the contemporary contention that belief in God is antithetical to intellectual rigor.

The tome at hand bespeaks not only to the devout and the scholar but alights upon the threshold of the skeptic. To those ensnared in doubt or cloaked in incredulity, it extends an olive branch, offering a path paved with reason and illuminated by faith.

Thomas Aquinas, whose intellect soared as the eagle, yet whose spirit was as humble as the sparrow, embarked on an odyssey that was both intellectual and spiritual. His was a journey that did not shun the world of thought in favor of blind faith, nor did it disdain the divine for the sake of reason. Instead, it wove these threads into a tapestry of theological and philosophical majesty.

This exposition explores the symbiosis of faith and reason, as epitomized by Aquinas, dispelling the myth that these realms exist in discord. Herein, we elucidate how Aquinas, with his monumental intellect, erected a fortress of faith, not on the sand of ignorance, but on the bedrock of reasoned belief.

To the scholars, theologians, and seekers of truth, this narrative is a clarion call to revisit the monumental life and works of Aquinas. It beckons us to ponder deeply the mysteries of faith, guided by the light of reason. For in the study of Aquinas, we find not only answers to perennial questions but also a stirring invitation to partake in the divine.

Through the prism of Thomistic thought, this work strives to persuade atheists and agnostics of the profound verity that Jesus is God. It endeavors to demonstrate how Aquinas, with unparalleled brilliance, argued for the existence of God with logical rigor and philosophical profundity.

In the unfolding of Aquinas's life, we discern the silhouette of a figure utterly committed to the pursuit of truth. From the cloisters of monastic life to the halls of academic discourse, his journey was marked by an insatiable quest for knowledge—knowledge that served not as an end but as a means to a higher, spiritual purpose.

The narrative held forth is not one of mere historical recounting but a call to spiritual awakening. It implores the reader to gaze through the lens of faith and reason, to see beyond the visible, and to grasp the hand that Aquinas extends across the ages.

Let this introduction serve not merely as a prelude to the life of a saint, but as a portal through which one might step from the shadows of doubt into the light of belief. For in the pages that follow, the reader is invited on a journey that transcends time, leading to the heart of divine truth, as revealed through the life and works of Thomas Aquinas.

In essence, this work is a testament to the undying brilliance of Aquinas's legacy—a legacy that continues to illuminate the path of faith for the skeptic, the student, the professor, and the devout. It is an ode to the harmony of faith and reason, a harmony that sings of divine truth and human understanding.

Thus, we embark on this exploration of Thomistic triumph, not as idle spectators but as active participants in a quest for enlightenment. For in the study of Aquinas, we do not merely learn of God; we come closer to understanding the divine essence that permeates our world and guides our intellects towards the ultimate truth.

So, let us commence, with keen minds and fervent hearts, to delve into the life and legacy of Thomas Aquinas. May this journey enrich our understanding, deepen our faith, and inspire a renewal of belief in those who have yet to see the light that Aquinas kindled so many centuries ago.

The Early Years of Thomas Aquinas

In the embrace of an era where the light of wisdom began to kindle anew within the hearts of men, there was birthed unto this realm a child who would grow to become a beacon of divine intellect and unwavering faith. Thomas Aquinas, born amidst the rolling hills of Aquino, came into this world bearing the legacy of his noble lineage; yet, it was not the clatter of swords nor the pursuit of worldly honor that called to his soul, but the silent whisper of the divine that beckoned him towards a life of contemplation and scholarly pursuit.

His early years, clothed in the rustic garments of innocence and curiosity, were a prelude to a symphony of theological revelation and philosophical inquiry. The domicile of his forebears, a crucible of familial expectation and societal duty, became both his refuge and his proving ground. Within its ancient walls, young Aquinas, nurtured by the nurturing hand of his mother, Theodora, began to display a voracious appetite for knowledge, his mind a fertile field ready to be sown with the seeds of wisdom.

The annals of his youth, though scant in the revelry and frivolity that oft accompany noble birth, were rich with the stirrings of a deep and abiding calling. As the world beyond the threshold of childhood beckoned, Thomas found himself at the crossroads of destiny, his heart aflame with a longing to serve not the fleeting crowns of earthly princes, but the eternal King of Kings. The decision to join the Dominicans, a bold defiance of his family's hopes, marked not only a pivotal moment in his own life but a turning point in the history of Christendom. For in embracing the mantle of mendicancy and scholarship, Aquinas embarked upon a journey that would lead him into the heart of sacred mystery and the depths of divine truth.

Thus did the early years of Thomas Aquinas unfold, a tapestry of trials and triumphs woven from the threads of grace and intellect. In the tender shoots of his burgeoning understanding, one might glimpse the promise of the towering oak he was destined to become—a man who would stand as a bridge between the earthly and the divine, whose life and works would forever testify to the harmonious concord of faith and reason.

The Birth of a Scholar

In the annals of history, seldom hast a moment so pivotal been marked, as when Thomas Aquinas, a beacon of intellect and faith, was birthed into this mortal coil. 'Twas in the year of our Lord twelve hundred and twenty-five, amidst the verdant landscapes of Italy, that Aquinas first drew breath, not knowing the magnitude his life would bear upon the world. From a lineage noble and keen of mind, young Aquinas was bestowed with the riches of education and faith, setting the stage for a journey extraordinary. Yet, 'twas not merely his birthright that foretold his scholarly destiny, but a fervor for knowledge and truth so potent, it could not be quenched. As a lad, he exhibited an insatiable curiosity and a wisdom beyond his years, traits that did portend the unparalleled scholastic pilgrimage he was to embark upon. Even in these nascent phases of life, Aquinas's profound questions and reflections on the divine hinted at his future role as a bridge between the realms of faith and reason, a herald of enlightenment in times oft-darkened by ignorance. And so, within the tapestry of history, the threads of Aquinas's early years were woven, marking the inception of a journey both spiritual and intellectual, the birth of a scholar destined to illuminate the minds and souls of many, leading them closer to the ineffable truth of our Creator.

Family Dynamics and Early Obstacles Within the annals of history, the tale of Thomas Aquinas unfolds, resembling a narrative of divine Providence interwoven with the mortal struggles of earthly existence. Born into the noble Aquino family, young Thomas was cradled not merely in wealth but also in a lineage that bore heavy expectations and formidable challenges. The Aquino household, bustling with the affairs of state and the clamor of many siblings, was a crucible within which the early life of Thomas was shaped.

His father, Count Landulf, a man of valor and prestige, envisioned a future for Thomas that would further elevate the family's stature. Likewise, his mother, Theodora, of equally noble lineage, harbored aspirations for her children that aligned with the grandeur of their heritage. In this environs of nobility, one might presume a life of ease and luxury for young Thomas; yet, 'twas not merely worldly riches and honors that the hand of fate had reserved for him.

The saga of Thomas's early years was beset with obstacles, both of external circumstance and internal turmoil. From his youngest days, the lad exhibited a disposition toward contemplation and study, often found in silent wonderment of the world's mysteries. Such inclinations did not wholly align with the martial and political aspirations his parents harbored for him.

The Aquino family, entrenched in the political machinations of the time, desired that Thomas would ascend to a prominent ecclesiastical position, one that would blend the temporal power of nobility with the spiritual influence of the Church. This intersection of ambition was not uncommon in an era where the fibers of religion and governance were closely knit. However, the young Aquinas harbored a deeper, more profound calling.

Adversity presented itself not only through familial expectations but also through the rigorous scholastic endeavors that young Thomas undertook. In an epoch where knowledge was a guarded treasure, the pursuit of scholastic excellence was fraught with hardship. Yet, it was within this crucible of study and the quest for understanding that Thomas's resolve was tempered.

At the tender age of five, Thomas was sent to the Abbey of Monte Cassino, a decision forged by his parents with dual motives: to commence his formal education and to pave the way for his future ascent within the Church hierarchy. 'Twas here, amidst the cloisters and the sacred quietude, that Thomas first encountered the vigorous life of the mind that would define his existence.

The Benedictine monks of Monte Cassino, guardians of knowledge and piety, became the first to nurture the ember of intellect within Thomas. Yet, even in this sanctified environment, the young scholar faced trials. The rigor of monastic discipline, the austerity of life within the abbey, and the expectation to excel cast shadows upon his path.

As Thomas grew in knowledge and stature, the external pressures mounted. His family's intentions for him to ascend within the ecclesiastical ranks of Monte Cassino began to clash with his emerging sense of divine calling. A calling not to power and influence but to truth and the service of the Almighty.

The shifting political landscapes of the time further complicated Thomas's journey. The fate of Monte Cassino, caught in the crossfire of conflicts between the Emperor and the Papacy, forced Thomas to depart. It was a juncture that marked the end of one chapter and the beginning of another. He was sent to the University of Naples, a move that unknowingly steered him towards his destiny.

In Naples, the intellectual fires within Thomas were stoked to new heights. Exposed to a broader curriculum, he encountered the works of Aristotle, a meeting of minds that would profoundly influence his theological and philosophical frameworks. However, Naples also introduced Thomas to the Dominicans, a meeting that would veer his life onto a path unforeseen by his family.

The decision to join the Dominicans, a mendicant order committed to poverty and preaching, was met with dismay and resistance from his family. Such a choice seemed antithetical to the ambitions they harbored for him. The ensuing conflict would test Thomas's resolve, pitting the call of divine service against familial duty and expectation.

Despite these tensions, Thomas's conviction remained unshaken. His commitment to follow his spiritual calling led to his clandestine departure to join the Dominicans. This act, perceived as a defiance of his family's wishes, set the stage for one of Thomas's greatest trials. His brothers, acting upon the family's behest, captured and imprisoned him in the family's castle, an ordeal that lasted for nearly a year.

Within the confinements of his captivity, Thomas's faith and resolve were put to the ultimate test. Yet, it was here, in the solitude and silence, that his dedication to his calling was purified and strengthened. Stories emerged of Thomas's unwavering commitment to his studies and his faith, even in the face of adversity and isolation.

At last, yielding to the force of his conviction and perhaps recognizing the futility of their opposition, Thomas's family relented. His release from captivity signified not only a physical liberation but also the vindication of his spiritual journey. This trial by fire had crystallized his resolve to dedicate his life to God and His truth.

Thus, the early obstacles and familial dynamics served not to deter Thomas Aquinas but to forge him into the scholar and saint he was destined to become. The trials he faced, both from without and within, honed his character and intellect, preparing him for the monumental works and theological insights that would shape the course of Christian thought for centuries to come.

Embracing the Call

In the tender years of his youth, amidst the verdant vales of Aquino, young Thomas found himself at the crossroads of divine destiny. The whispers of the Lord beckoned unto him, a gentle yet irrefutable summons to forsake the riches and renown that birthright and lineage promised. Amidst familial furore and societal skepticism, the stark, unadorned life of the Dominicans drew his soul with an ineluctable pull. Forsooth, it was not merely a rejection of worldly pomp and princely privilege that spurred him; 'twas a heartfelt embracing of a higher calling, a sacred vocation that promiseth a fusion of intellect and immutable faith. Herein, the nascent inklings of his destiny unfurled, as Thomas Aquinas, swayed not by the tempests of external dissent, chose the path less trod - a testament to the strength and purity of his consecrated intent. This decision to join the Order of Preachers marked the dawning of a journey profound, a consecration of life to the pursuit of truth through the lens of divine revelation, setting the stage for a legacy that would kindle the light of faith and reason across the annals of time.

The Decision to Join the Dominicans In the tapestry of ecclesiastical history, few threads are woven with as much providence and purpose as the life choice of Thomas Aquinas to embrace the Dominican order. This pivotal moment, shrouded in the divine mystery of calling, was not merely an act of personal piety but a corner stone laid for the edification of the Church and the enrichment of Christian thought.

The sage Aquinas, in his youth, found himself at a crossroads, the kind which determines not just the course of one's life, but through which the history of the Church itself might be channeled. His decision was not made lightly, nor was it met with universal acclaim. For, in choosing the path of a mendicant friar, he eschewed not only the material wealth and status proffered by his noble lineage but also the expectations of his kinsmen, who envisioned for him a prestigious ecclesiastical career.

Ere we delve deeper into this decision, let us consider the world in which Thomas found himself. It was a time when the Church sought desperately to navigate between the Scylla of burgeoning heresies and the Charybdis of secular encroachments. In this tumultuous sea, the Dominicans emerged as a beacon of hope, committed to preaching, teaching, and the defense of the True Faith.

Founded by Saint Dominic, the Order of Preachers was conceived out of a profound zeal for the salvation of souls. The friars took to heart the apostolic mission, venturing forth without silver or gold, armed only with the Gospel and their intellects to win hearts for Christ. It was this zeal that kindled a flame in Thomas's heart—a flame that would not be quenched by the lure of temporal prestige or comfort.

Moreover, the scholarly tradition of the Dominicans provided fertile ground for Thomas's burgeoning intellect. The order was not only dedicated to the pastoral care of souls but also to the rigorous pursuit of truth through study. This dual commitment resonated deeply with Thomas, for whom the love of God and the love of learning were inseparable.

Yet, the path to his vocation was fraught with trials. His family, dismayed by his decision, endeavored to sway his resolve, employing both entreaties and confinement. The struggle between the call of blood and the call of the spirit tore at Thomas's heart, yet it was through this crucible that his determination was refined and his vocation affirmed.

Legend holds that during his confinement, Thomas was subjected to a final test of his resolve—a temptation of the flesh. His reaction was not one of fear or anger but of serene confidence in his calling. Seizing a burning brand, he etched a cross upon the wall of his cell, a symbol of his unwavering commitment to Christ and his vow of chastity. Henceforth, he was undisturbed, the heavenly hosts, it is said, guarding him as he rested.

When at last he was released, it was not into a life of comfort and ease that Thomas stepped, but into one of poverty, peripatetic toil, and unparalleled intellectual labor. In the habit of the Dominicans, he found not a mark of worldly abasement but a garment of freedom. Free to pursue truth wherever it might lead, free to serve the Church in humility and faith, free to love God with all his mind and heart.

His entrance into the Dominican order was not merely an act of joining a religious community; it was an assent to a life of radical discipleship. Thomas embraced the mendicant way of life, its rigors and its riches alike. He walked the path of voluntary poverty, relying on divine providence and the charity of others, that he might be rich in faith and wisdom.

Through his choice, Thomas became a bridge between the monastic and scholarly traditions, embodying the Dominican ideal of contemplata aliis tradere—to pass on to others the fruits of contemplation. His life and works stand as a testament to the idea that faith and reason, far from being adversaries, are allies in the pursuit of truth.

Indeed, the decision to join the Dominicans was more than a personal choice; it was a pivotal moment in the history of Christian thought. In the cloisters and lecture halls of the order, Thomas's intellect found both challenge and encouragement. His mentors and brethren, particularly the illustrious Albertus Magnus, recognized in him a mind capable of synthesizing revelation and reason, a task to which he devoted his life with unwavering zeal.

Thus, Thomas's choice was not simply about which habit to don, but about what kind of scholar, what kind of saint, he aspired to be. His ensuing works, particularly the Summa Theologica, serve not only as a monument to his genius but as a beacon of light for those who seek to navigate the waters of faith and reason.

In reflection, the decision to join the Dominicans was not merely a turning point in the life of Thomas Aquinas; it was a moment of grace, through which God worked to bring about a profound renewal in the Church. Through his writings, teachings, and the example of his life, Thomas continues to instruct, inspire, and intercede for us, demonstrating that the love of truth and the love of God are one and the same.

Thus, let us hold fast to the legacy of Saint Thomas Aquinas, remembering that in the pursuits of the mind and the yearnings of the heart, we are ever guided by divine providence. In the story of his life and vocation, we find not only an exemplar of holiness but an invitation to each of us to embrace our own callings with courage, humility, and love.

The Journey to Enlightenment

In the quest for divine truth, Thomas Aquinas embarked upon a journey that would illuminate the corridors of his mind with the light of scholarly pursuit and devout faith. His path to enlightenment, a tale as rich and complex as the tapestries of yore, began with his footsteps echoing through the halls of academia in Paris and Cologne. 'Twas in these seats of learning, under the watchful gaze of luminous minds, that the fabric of his intellect was woven with threads of ancient wisdom and celestial contemplation. It was here, amidst the tomes and parchments, that Aquinas encountered Albertus Magnus, a beacon of knowledge whose mentorship kindled the nascent spark within Thomas into a flame that would light the way for others. This spiritual and intellectual awakening, marked by rigorous study and contemplative prayer, was not merely a pursuit of knowledge for knowledge's sake, but a sacred mission to harmonize the truths of faith with the discoveries of reason.

As Aquinas trod this scholarly path, his soul was stirred by the profound mysteries of existence, leading him to contemplations vast and deep. His journey was one of transformation—where intellect met divinity, and where reason and faith embraced in a celestial dance. This odyssey, fraught with challenges and illuminated by moments of epiphany, was not an endeavor undertaken in isolation. It was a pilgrimage shared with fellow seekers of truth, a testament to the enduring quest for enlightenment that beckons to each soul inclined towards the divine. In this chapter, 'tis the tale of Aquinas's journey to enlightenment we recount —a journey that stands as a beacon to all who seek to navigate the tempestuous seas of doubt and to anchor in the harbor of transcendent truth.

The Scholarly Path

In the annals of history, where intellect and spirit entwine, Thomas Aquinas embarked upon a journey most divine. Within the hallowed halls of Paris and Cologne, his mind, like a star in the darkest night, brightly shone. 'Twas not merely the acquisition of wisdom sought; but a fervent quest to intertwine the threads of thought with the very essence of faith's tapestry. Aquinas, in his pursuit, did not shy from philosophy nor the rigorous scrutiny of theology. Each tome, each scripture, each discourse with scholars of yore, propelled him not towards a mere earthly lore but towards a celestial understanding, a binding of soul and intellect that transcends mortal stand. His path was not laid in mere academic pursuit but forged in the crucible of divine truth, where knowledge serves not as master but as faithful servant to faith's unwavering light. Thus, through scholastic endeavour and divine grace, Aquinas sought to unveil the visage of the Almighty, proving that in the heart of true wisdom, faith doth brightly burn, guiding the wayward and the lost to the embrace of the Eternal.

Studies in Paris and Cologne In the tapestry of Medieval Christendom, where threads of faith and reason intertwine with the warp and weft of learning, the journey of Thomas Aquinas stands as a testament to the pursuit of enlightenment. Thrust from the nurturing cradle of his familial hearth, young Thomas set forth unto Paris, a city teeming with the ferment of intellectual rigor, where scholars and students congregated like moths to the flame of knowledge. Here, amidst the Gothic splendor of its edifices, he would immerse himself in the studious life, a life dedicated to the piercing of nature's veils through the power of reason, guided ever by the light of faith.

In this venerable city, where the Seine whispers tales of yore to those who would listen, Thomas found himself at the University of Paris. It was a place as daunting as it was inspiring, a crucible for the shaping of minds. The air was alive with the dialectics of logic, the poetry of philosophy, and the fervor of theology. Students and masters alike engaged in vigorous debate, their discourse a tapestry of inquiry and affirmation, of questioning and understanding. In this arena, Thomas, undaunted by the enormity of the task before him, began to forge the tools of his intellectual craft.

Yet, it was not in Paris alone that his scholarly journey would unfold. In due course, Providence would guide him to Cologne, where the shadow of Albertus Magnus, a figure of towering intellect and piety, loomed large. Under the tutelage of this venerable master, Thomas was to delve deeper into the mysteries of creation, his mind and soul being shaped by the disciplines of philosophy and theology, intertwined as the vine that embraces the trellis. Albertus, perceiving the luminous intelligence and the unquenchable thirst for truth in his pupil, imparted to Thomas not only the knowledge accumulated over ages but also the wisdom to discern the divine within the mundane.

Paris and Cologne thus served as the anvil and hammer in the shaping of Thomas Aquinas's intellect. In Paris, he wrestled with the legacy of Aristotle, whose works, recently re-introduced to the West, challenged the Christian intellectuals to reconcile pagan philosophy with the truth of the Gospel. It was a task that demanded not only intellectual acuity but also a profound faith in the capacity of human reason to grasp the divine. Thomas rose to this challenge, his mind a forge where faith and reason were melded into a coherent whole.

Amidst the cloisters of Cologne, under Albertus's guidance, Thomas's understanding of the natural world and the divine principles that govern it deepened. Here, the studies were imbued with a sense of the sacred, a reminder that all pursuit of knowledge is but a journey towards the Creator. The teachings of Albertus, rich in breadth and depth, spanned the speculative and the practical, the mundane and the mystical, preparing Thomas for the monumental task that lay ahead.

As the seasons turned, so did Thomas's studies progress. The volumes of Aristotle, the scriptures, and the writings of the Church Fathers were grist to his intellectual mill. With each passing day, his understanding grew, his insights deepened, and his ability to synthesize the disparate threads of thought into a coherent tapestry of belief and understanding became ever more apparent. His fellow students, a congregation of future scholars, theologians, and clergy, looked on in awe as Thomas, with humility and grace, navigated the complexities of debate and discourse.

In the course of his studies, Thomas encountered opposition and skepticism from those who saw in Aristotle's works a threat to Christian orthodoxy. Yet, with a heart steadfast in faith and a mind sharp as a scholar's quill, he ventured forth into the fray, defending the integration of faith and reason as complementary paths to truth. In Paris, the academic skirmishes in which he engaged honed his rhetorical skills and deepened his resolve to pursue truth, wherever it might lead.

The confines of lecture halls and scriptoria were not the only places where Thomas sought understanding. Paris itself, a microcosm of the medieval world, provided a vibrant backdrop against which his intellectual and spiritual journey unfolded. The city's churches, its poor, and its art all spoke to Thomas, informing his understanding of God's presence in the world and the nature of humanity's relationship with the divine.

In Cologne, the rhythm of monastic life added another dimension to his studies. The daily round of prayer and work, the communal reading of scripture, the quiet contemplation of nature's beauty—these practiced in the hush of dawn or the still of night, enriched Thomas's soul, weaving a deeper spirituality into the fabric of his thought.

Thus, through years of diligent study in Paris and Cologne, through debates and discussions, through prayer and meditation, Thomas Aquinas's intellect and spirit were honed. He emerged from this period not merely as a scholar of repute but as a beacon of faith, reason, and understanding. In his hands, the legacy of Aristotle was not a challenge to Christian thought but a tool for deepening the understanding of the divine mystery.

It was in these cities that Thomas's foundational beliefs were tested and tempered. His conviction that faith and reason were not adversaries but allies in the quest for truth became the cornerstone of his theological and philosophical inquiries. Here in the crucibles of Paris and Cologne, Thomas Aquinas crafted the intellectual weapons with which he would engage the heresies and misunderstandings of his day, advocating for a faith that was both enlightened by reason and enriching to it.

The years spent in Paris and Cologne were but chapters in the larger story of Thomas Aquinas's life. Yet, they were pivotal, for they laid the foundation upon which he would build his monumental contributions to theology and philosophy. In the bustling streets of Paris and the quiet cloisters of Cologne, he had forged his intellect in the fire of academic rigor, tempered it with the waters of spiritual insight, and emerged prepared to illuminate the world with the light of his thought.

It is to this journey of mind and spirit that we owe the treasures of Thomistic thought. In the hallowed halls of learning and the sanctified spaces of prayer, Thomas Aquinas proved that the quest for knowledge, guided by faith, can lead the soul to glimpse the face of God. This story, rooted in the past, speaks still to our present, reminding us that within the heart of true learning burns the light of divine truth.

And so, the saga of Thomas's studies in Paris and Cologne concluded, but the legacy of his intellectual pilgrimage—a journey of faith seeking understanding—continues to inspire those who, in our own times, tread the paths of scholarship and spirituality. In the narrative of Thomas Aquinas's formative years, we find a beacon that guides us through the tempests of doubt and disbelief, toward the harbor of truth witnessed in the person of Jesus, the Christ.

Encounters with Albertus Magnus

In the tapestry of Thomas' journey, the weft encountered the warp in a fateful meeting with Albertus Magnus, a learned master whose intellect and spirit were as a beacon of light in the darkened room of inquiry. Within the hallowed halls of Cologne, where the air itself seemed imbued with the thirst for knowledge, Thomas found himself under the tutelage of Albertus, a mentor who recognized the latent spark within the young scholar. 'Twas under his guidance that Thomas' philosophical and theological musings were honed, much like a blade upon the whetstone. Albertus, a visionary who straddled the realms of faith and reason with ease, was instrumental in shepherding Thomas through the labyrinth of scholastic thought. In debates, arms intertwined in intellectual combat, Albertus led by example, illustrating the power that lay in the symbiosis of divine grace and human understanding. This period was a crucible, forging Thomas' resolve and illuminating the path that lay before him. 'Twas an awakening, a shift from the shadows of doubt to the luminescence of certainty, guided by the steady hand of Albertus Magnus, whose influence upon Thomas was as the imprint upon clay, shaping his student into a vessel fit to carry forth the light of knowledge and faith.

Mentorship and Intellectual Awakening In the tapestry of the storied life of Thomas Aquinas, threads of gold are interwoven, representing the luminaries who mentored and shaped his burgeoning intellect. Among the plethora of influences, the figure of Albertus Magnus stands as a tower of erudition, casting a long shadow across the landscape of Aquinas's intellectual formation. It was under the aegis of Albertus that Aquinas was to experience an awakening that would steer him onto the path of scholastic prominence.

In the verdant valleys of Cologne, amidst the cloisters that hummed with scholarly pursuits, Aquinas found himself under the tutelage of Albertus. This mentorship was not merely about the transfer of knowledge; it was a forging of character and intellect in the crucible of divine wisdom. For Albertus was no ordinary mentor; he was a beacon of enlightenment in an age seeking direction, a man whose intellect traversed the breadth of human knowledge and whose spirit sought the divine in all things.

Within these hallowed halls, a profound transformation began. Aquinas, whose mind was as an uncultivated field, rich in potential but lacking in form, found in Albertus the guide who would help till and tend his intellectual soil. Their discourse spanned the gamut of philosophical inquiry; from the essence of being to the nature of the divine, no stone was left unturned in their quest for understanding.

The influence of Albertus on Aquinas was not confined to the boundaries of philosophy. It extended into theology, a realm where faith and reason danced in a delicate balance. Albertus instilled in Aquinas a reverence for the ancient texts, showing him how the wisdom of the past could illuminate the challenges of the present. He taught his protégé the importance of asking questions, of doubting, and, most crucially, of believing.

Under the mentorship of Albertus, Aquinas came to perceive the interconnectedness of all knowledge. He saw how the laws that governed the natural world were but reflections of a higher order, a divine symmetry that underpinned the universe. This epiphany was to become a cornerstone of his philosophical and theological edifice.

The lessons were rigorous, demanding a level of dedication and discipline that few could muster. Yet, Aquinas, with a zeal fueled by a quest for divine truth, rose to the challenge. He imbibed not just the knowledge that Albertus offered, but also the method and manner of his inquiry. It was this intellectual rigor, combined with a steadfast faith, that was to become the hallmark of Aquinas's work.

The mentorship was, however, not a one-way street. Albertus, in Aquinas, found not just a student but a kindred spirit, a mind as eager and capable as his own. Their dialogues, rich with the wisdom of the ancients and the freshness of new discovery, were as iron sharpening iron. In these exchanges, both mentor and protégé were refined.

It was during these formative years that Aquinas began to develop his most enduring contributions to theology and philosophy. The seeds planted by Albertus, watered with diligent study and deep reflection, began to sprout. The notions of the Summa Theologica, his magnum opus, were conceived in the fertile ground of this mentorship.

The relationship between Albertus and Aquinas serves as a testament to the transformative power of mentorship. It was a partnership that transcended the conventional boundaries of teacher and student, rooted in a mutual pursuit of truth. Their collaboration was a beacon of intellectual and spiritual awakening in an era hungering for both.

In the shadow of Albertus, Aquinas learned the importance of humility. He saw in his mentor a model of how to wield intellect and wisdom not as tools for personal aggrandizement but as gifts in the service of God and humanity. This lesson, perhaps more than any other, was to define Aquinas's approach to his life's work.

The legacy of this mentorship extends far beyond the immediate contributions of both men to scholarship. It serves as a blueprint for intellectual inquiry, a demonstration of how faith and reason can coexist and complement each other. In their exchange, we find the embodiment of a scholarly pursuit that does not shy away from the divine but instead embraces it as the source of all wisdom.

Thus, in the chronicles of Thomas Aquinas's journey to enlightenment, the chapter on his mentorship under Albertus Magnus occupies a place of honor. It was a period that not only shaped his intellectual pursuits but also his spiritual path. The lessons learned, the wisdom shared, became the foundation upon which Aquinas would build his legacy.

In retrospect, the mentorship between Albertus and Aquinas encapsulates the essence of the intellectual awakening that marked the medieval era. It was a time when minds of great capacity sought to reconcile the seen with the unseen, the empirical with the mystical. Their dialogue, steeped in mutual respect and a shared longing for the divine, stands as a beacon to those who seek to navigate the complex interplay between faith and reason.

The tale of mentorship and intellectual awakening between Albertus Magnus and Thomas Aquinas is not merely a chapter in the annals of history. It is a narrative that continues to inspire, a reminder of the heights to which the human spirit can soar when anchored in faith and guided by wisdom. In their story, we find not just the roots of Thomistic thought but a timeless guide for our own intellectual and spiritual journeys.

In this manner, the mentorship and intellectual awakening of Thomas Aquinas under the guidance of Albertus Magnus stands as a testament to the enduring power of divine wisdom, guiding the hand of man in his unceasing quest for understanding. Let us take heed of their example, pursuing knowledge with a vigor tempered by humility and a heart open to the whispers of the divine. Thus, may we too walk the path of enlightenment, our steps guided by the light of faith and reason intertwined.

The Essence of Thomistic Theology

In the annals of Christian thought, few have pierced the veil 'twixt faith and reason with such acuity as Thomas Aquinas, whose theologic endeavors blend the ethereal with the tangible, seeking ever to unveil the Divine through the prism of human understanding. Within this chapter lies the heart of Thomistic theology, a sacred confluence where belief and intellect converge, not as adversaries, but as allies in the pursuit of truth. Aquinas, with a mind both vast and deep, proposes that the mortal quest for knowledge, far from leading souls astray, guides them nearer to the celestial throne. Through his celebrated Five Ways, Aquinas ventures to prove God's existence, employing the tools of philosophy to illuminate the path to spiritual enlightenment. This chapter, thus, stands not merely as a treatise but as a beacon, a testament to the belief that faith, fortified by reason, reveals a higher order, one in which the mysteries of the Divine become not less mysterious, but more profoundly grasped and cherished by the minds and hearts of those who seek.

Faith and Reason: A Harmonious Relationship

In the labyrinthine journey towards understanding, where the mind oft doth wander amidst shadows of doubt and towers of questions, the teachings of Thomas Aquinas stand as a beacon of harmony between faith and reason. 'Tis a misconception, old as time, that these two must be at odds, like two knights in ceaseless battle. Yet, Aquinas proclaimed a truth most sublime: faith and reason, far from foes, are the twin stars guiding humanity's quest for knowledge and divine truth. He, with the mastery of a skilled artisan, wove together the threads of Aristotelian philosophy and Christian theology, showing that reason, with its probing questions and relentless logic, can pave the way to faith, while faith can elevate reason beyond the bounds of earthly understanding. This harmony, 'tis not a mere truce, but a profound union that lifts the soul towards the heavens, proving that the pursuit of knowledge, guided by reason, serves to deepen one's love and understanding of the divine. In Aquinas's vision, the mind's journey is not a solitary ramble, but a pilgrimage shared with God, where every insight gleaned through reason is but a step closer to the divine mystery, and faith is the light that illuminates the path. Such is the essence of Thomistic theology—a harmonious symphony of faith and reason, playing a melody that leads the inquiring soul to the very heart of divine truth.

Debunking the Myth of Conflict Within the annals of history, oft hath it been proclaimed—by skeptic and believer alike—that a great chasm lies betwixt faith and reason, as if the two were naught but star-crossed lovers, fated never to conjoin. This, however, is a misconception most grievous, and one that our esteemed Thomas Aquinas sought earnestly to dispel. For in his wisdom, he did see that faith and reason, far from being adversaries, are allies in the quest for truth.

Consider ye the nature of faith: it asks of us to believe in that which lies beyond the reach of our senses, to trust in the unseen. Reason, meanwhile, demands evidence, seeks understanding through observation and logic. At a glance, these two might seem at odds, yet Aquinas did argue, with meticulous precision, that they are but two paths leading toward the same ultimate truth. Thus, in his grand vision, conflict between them is not only needless but unnatural.

Many a scholar hath argued that to rely on faith alone is folly, for it leads one into the realms of superstition and myth. Others, with equal vehemence, have contended that reason alone suffices not, for it can explain the how but not the why, the mechanics but not the meaning. Aquinas, with a scholar's acuity and a mystic's insight, bridged these disparate views, presenting a synthesis where faith informs reason and reason deepens faith.

Take, for instance, his famous exposition on the existence of God, wherein he put forth five proofs not as mere declarations of faith but as logical arguments that appeal to reason. Through natural observations and philosophical discourse, he sought not to coerce but to convince, to show that belief in God could withstand the scrutiny of reason.

In his voluminous writings, one doth detect an undercurrent of profound respect for both divine revelation and human inquiry. He didst not shy from engaging with the works of Aristotle, Avicenna, and other great minds, regardless of their spiritual inclinations. Indeed, he saw in their quest for knowledge a reflection of his own, believing that all truth, irrespective of its source, ultimately leads to God.

This harmony between faith and reason, as expounded by Aquinas, doth challenge the prevailing notion of their conflict. 'Tis a stance of remarkable foresight, arguing that truth, whether unveiled through Divine Revelation or discovered through human reason, is of a single essence. Hence, the pursuit of understanding, be it through theological study or empirical investigation, is not a divergence but a convergence towards comprehending the divine nature of our existence.

Moreover, Aquinas' approach serves as a beacon for those embroiled in the contemporary discourses that often pit science against religion. By demonstrating that reason can lead to faith and faith can enlighten reason, he offers a model for dialogue and integration rather than division and discord. His works stand as a testament to the possibility of intellectual rigor coupled with spiritual devotion.

In the intricate tapestry of Aquinas' thought, one finds no trace of the simplistic dichotomy that characterizes modern debates on faith and reason. Instead, there is a profound unity, a belief in the complementarity of different ways of knowing. This vision is both liberating and demanding, for it requires of us an openness to truth, regardless of the guise under which it presents itself.

To dismiss Aquinas' synthesis of faith and reason as mere theological idealism would be to overlook the profound impact of his ideas on the development of Western thought. Throughout the ages, his influence has permeated discussions on morality, science, and law, proving that his reconciliation of faith and reason was not only philosophically robust but practically applicable.

Indeed, amidst the tumults of our times, where extremism in the guise of faith or reason wreaks havoc upon societies, Aquinas' teachings offer a haven of wisdom. His insistence on the compatibility of faith and reason provides a bulwark against the twin terrors of fanaticism and nihilism, both of which threaten the fabric of our communal life.

Thus, to engage with Aquinas is to embark upon a journey that transcends the simplistic binaries of faith versus reason. It is to explore a landscape where intellect and spirit walk hand in hand, where the mysteries of faith are not obstacles to reason, but invitations to deeper understanding.

If the myth of conflict between faith and reason is to be finally put to rest, it shall be through a renewed appreciation of Aquinas' vision. For in his writings, we are reminded that truth, in its ultimate form, is neither solely a matter of empirical proof nor blind belief, but a symphony in which reason and faith each have their part to play.

Therefore, let us forsake the notion of an inherent conflict between faith and reason as a relic of an unenlightened past. With Aquinas as our guide, let us forge ahead into a future where the luminous rays of truth dispel the shadows of misunderstanding and division. For verily, in the harmonious relationship between faith and reason lies the key to unlocking the deepest mysteries of our existence and of the divine.

In this endeavor, let us recall the words of Aquinas himself, who saw the quest for knowledge as a sacred journey towards the divine. In his pursuit of truth, Aquinas serves not only as a beacon of intellectual and spiritual enlightenment but as a bridge between worlds, cultures, and epochs. He stands as a paragon of the unity of knowledge, a testament to the enduring power of faith illuminated by reason.

Thus, in the final reckoning, when history doth look upon the legacy of Thomas Aquinas, it shall not behold a figure ensnared in the dichotomy of faith against reason, but rather a luminary who transcended such divisions. In his monumental work and life, Aquinas embodied the profound, enduring, and transformative synthesis of faith and reason. This singular achievement challenges us, across the ages, to view them not as foes but as the twin stars guiding humanity's voyage through the vast expanse of knowledge and belief.

The Five Ways: Proving God's Existence

In the annals of theological discourse, there hath scarcely been a mind so acute, nor an argument so compelling, as those proffered by Thomas Aquinas in his quest to bridge the chasm 'twixt faith and reason. It is within the hallowed pages of his magnum opus, the Summa Theologica, that we find the Five Ways - Aquinas's venerable attempt to prove the existence of God, not by faith alone, but through the clear light of reason.

The first of these paths, the Argument from Motion, posits that all things in motion can trace their impetus back to a First Mover – one uncaused and immutable, who set the cosmos into its perpetual dance. For, can a thing bring itself into motion from a standstill? Verily, it cannot; thus, we must conclude that a Prime Mover doth exist, whom we recognize as God.

Next, Aquinas presents the Argument from Causation, contending that in this realm of existence, nothing can be the cause of itself. It stands to reason, then, that there must needs be a First Cause – uncaused, itself – which begets all subsequent chains of causation. This Uncaused Cause, Aquinas avers, is God.

His third way, known as the Argument from Contingency, reflects upon the nature of beings that are contingent – that is, those whose existence is not necessary. Given that contingent beings are and then are not, if at any time there were naught but contingent beings, there would have been a time when nothing existed. Out of naught, naught comes; thus, there must exist a Necessary Being through whom all contingency finds its genesis. This being, Aquinas identifies as God.

The fourth way is the Argument from Gradation, observing the gradations of perfection found in the world. There are varying degrees of goodness, truth, nobility, and the like, which we measure in relation to the highest degree of these qualities. This presupposes the existence of a maximum, an ultimate source of goodness and perfection – and this, he asserts, we call God.

Lastly, the Argument from Final Cause or Teleology, asserts that non-intelligent entities work towards an end or purpose. This evident order cannot be attributed to chance but must be directed by one who understands the end toward which all things aim. This director of all natural purposes is also God.

Each of these paths, though separate and distinct in their reasoning, converge upon a singular truth: the existence of a transcendent being, God, who is the primal cause and final end of all things. Aquinas's enterprise, fraught with the rigor of philosophical inquiry, seeks to illumine our understanding and guide our reason to behold that which faith hath already embraced.

Yet, in laying out these arguments, Aquinas does not merely assert dominion of reason over faith, but rather illuminates the symbiotic dance 'twixt the two. For in the heart of the believer, reason and faith do not quarrel, but enrich one another, guiding the soul closer to the divine. Aquinas's Five Ways serve not as a demand for unyielding assent but as an invitation to embark upon a journey of understanding, wherein the traveler is met with signs of God's existence, writ large upon the tapestry of creation.

This intellectual voyage, whilst challenging, is profoundly rewarding. For within the framework of Aquinas's arguments lies an implicit call to ponder not just the abstract existence of God, but His active and ongoing relationship with all creation. The Prime Mover still moves, the First Cause still acts, the Necessary Being sustains, the Ultimate Good draws all to Himself, and the Final Cause directs all things towards their end.

In the telling of these Five Ways, Aquinas offers not only proofs but also a profound meditation on the nature of existence itself. He invites us to contemplate the world around us, to observe the movements, the causes, the contingencies, the gradations, and the purposes that pervade all things. In each, he intimates the presence of the divine, calling us to a deeper awareness of the constant interaction between the created and the Creator.

Thus, in pondering Aquinas's Five Ways, the devout and the doubtful alike are beckoned to look beyond the veil of the material, to the ultimate realities that lie beyond our sight. Aquinas, with the keenness of his intellect and the depth of his faith, serves as a beacon of light, leading souls to the shores of divine truth.

Indeed, the Five Ways are more than mere arguments; they are a testament to a mind enamored by God, striving to articulate the inexpressible, to make known the unknowable, and to bring souls closer to the unfathomable mystery of the divine. In this endeavor, Aquinas stands as a colossus, straddling the realms of faith and reason, calling each of us to venture forth on the path to enlightenment and ultimately, to God Himself.

Let us, therefore, with minds open and hearts aflame, delve into the teachings of Aquinas, allowing the light of his wisdom to guide us in our quest for understanding. May the journey along these Five Ways not only illumine the truth of God's existence but inspire within us a deeper love for the One who is the source of all being, the summit of all good, and the final end of our desires.

In conclusion, Thomas Aquinas's Five Ways, meticulously wrought in the crucible of reason, stand as enduring beacons of faith's compatibility with reason. They invite us not to a blind faith, but to one that seeks, questions, and ultimately finds rest in the incomprehensible majesty of God. Through these paths, Aquinas has indelibly marked the journey of countless souls towards the divine, proving himself not just a theologian of his time, but a guide for all ages, leading us ever closer to the heart of the eternal.

A Life of Mendicancy and Devotion

Within the cloisters of dominion, wherein the brethren of St. Dominic tread the path of humility and sacrifice, did Thomas Aquinas choose to render himself unto a life marked by the absence of earthly treasures, seeking instead the richness of divine wisdom and closeness to the Almighty. This choice, a profound testament to his faith, distinguished him not merely as a scholar of highest repute but as a friar wholly devoted to the service of God and His creation. His days, filled with the solemnity of prayer, the rigors of preaching, and the communal life of piety, served as a beacon of light unto those ensnared by the shadows of doubt and disbelief. Through mendicancy, Thomas embraced a life void of material possession, thereby casting off the shackles of worldly desire to journey unencumbered towards spiritual enlightenment and divine truth. His devotion knew no bounds, for in the pews of the impoverished and the halls of the learned alike, he sought to sow the seeds of faith, arguing not from a place of arrogance but of profound humility and unshakeable belief in the Lord's providence. It was through this harmonious blend of destitution and devout faith that Thomas Aquinas endeavored to bridge the chasm betwixt reason and revelation, proving, through the very testament of his life, that true wisdom and understanding are but servants to the grandeur of faith in Jesus Christ, the Son of God.

The Choice of Poverty

In the grand tapestry of his life, Thomas Aquinas chose a path less trodden, a vow of poverty over the opulence his noble birth might have afforded him. This choice, neither trifling nor made with lightness of heart, bespoke a devotion profound and earnest. Herein lay a man, not swayed by gold or earthly dominion, but driven by a relentless pursuit of divine truth and spiritual riches. The mendicant's cloak he donned was not a mark of penury but a royal garb of freedom from worldly chains, enabling him to delve into the mysteries of faith with singular focus. Yea, for Aquinas, the relinquishment of earthly possessions was no mere renunciation but a joyful embrace of a life suffused with divine purpose. Each day, as he broke bread with his brethren, the nobility of his spirit shone brighter, a beacon to all who sought to reconcile the terrestrial with the celestial. His choice, verily, was not a retreat from the world but an invitation to discover the infinite within the finite, a testament to the belief that true wealth lieth not in the abundance of possessions, but in the richness of the soul attuned to the divine will.

Rejecting Worldly Riches for Spiritual Wealth As we venture forth from the chronicles of the early years of Thomas Aquinas, let us embark upon a contemplation most profound, concerning the rejection of earthly treasures for the attainment of heavenly riches.

In an epoch when many a soul did equate wealth with divine blessing, and poverty with divine disfavor, Thomas, guided by the light of Divine Wisdom, chose a path less trodden. He discerned, with keen intellect and a heart aflame with love for the Almighty, that true treasure lay not in gold nor lands vast, but in the riches of the soul, nurtured by grace and virtue.

'Twas a choice most daring, for Thomas hailed from a lineage noble and expectations grand surrounded his future. Yet, he spurned these callings worldly, for a call divine whispered to his heart's core. He saw beyond the transient allure of opulence, envisioning instead a kingdom not of this world, where wealth is measured in piety and devotion.

To embrace such a path required not merely a forsaking of material wealth, but a profound transformation of being. Thomas adopted a life of mendicancy, joining the Order of Preachers, known as the Dominicans, whose charism it is to live in poverty, preach the Gospel, and study scripture and theology for the salvation of souls.

In his robe simple and sandals worn, Thomas became a testament to the strength of spiritual conviction over worldly desire. He wandered not in palaces grand, but in halls of learning and chapels humble, where his heart found its truest joy in communion with the Divine.

The road he chose was fraught with challenge, for not all eyes saw the worth in a life devoted to poverty and academic pursuit. Yet, Thomas stood firm, a beacon of light guiding toward a truth oft-forgotten — that to gain all, one must be willing to lose all.

It behooves us to pause and ponder — what is it that we value? Are our hearts set upon wealth that moth and rust doth corrupt, or upon treasures of the spirit, everlasting? Thomas Aquinas, in his life and works, offers a resounding answer. He chose the latter, for in his wisdom he perceived that spiritual wealth sufficeth to content the heart, rendering unnecessary an overabundance of worldly goods.

Moreover, Thomas's rejection of earthly riches for spiritual wealth was not a mere personal choice devoid of wider implication. Nay, 'twas a profound statement on the nature of true happiness and fulfillment. He demonstrated through his life's work that knowledge, when wielded in the service of faith, becomes a conduit of divine grace, enriching the soul beyond measure.

This transformation from worldly wealth to spiritual richness also manifested in his teachings and writings. Thomas fervently argued that the ultimate end of human existence is not found in the accumulation of wealth, but in beatitude — seeing God face to face. Wealth and possessions, he maintained, should serve this ultimate purpose, as means rather than ends in themselves.

Yet, let it not be said that Thomas spurned the world entirely, for he embraced creation as a reflection of the Creator's grandeur. His aim was not to decry the world, but to elevate the gaze of humanity toward the source of true good, true beauty, and true wealth.

In a society oft seduced by the sheen of gold and the whisper of fame, Thomas Aquinas stands as a testament to a profound truth: that contentment resides not in possessions manifold, but in the richness of a soul aligned with its Creator.

The narrative of his life invites us, then, to reflect upon our own pursuits. Do we heed the call of worldly wealth, or do we strive for spiritual riches that neither tarnish nor fade? In the fabric of our daily endeavors, let us weave threads of charity, humility, and piety, amassing wealth untold in the treasury of Heaven.

In sum, Thomas Aquinas's choice to eschew temporal riches for the sake of spiritual wealth was not a denial of the world, but an affirmation of a higher calling. His life serves as a beacon, illuminating a path of renunciation that leads to the truest form of enrichment — union with the Divine.

Therefore, as we forge ahead in our own journeys, may we draw inspiration from Thomas's example, choosing always the path of virtue over vice, the eternal over the ephemeral. For in the end, the riches of this world will fade, but the wealth of the spirit endures forevermore.

Let us, then, with hearts emboldened by faith and minds enlightened by reason, pursue not the riches that eye can see, but those unseen; for therein lies the true wealth, the treasure imperishable, that Thomas Aquinas, in his wisdom and sanctity, chose above all else.

Day-to-Day Life as a Friar

In the monastic cloisters where the friars of mendicancy dwell, each day unfurls as a tapestry woven with threads of devotion and duty. Ere the sun doth kiss the horizon, these humble servants of the Lord wake to the solemn call of matins, their voices rising in a chorus that sanctifies the morn. The cloister halls, scant adorned and echoing with the footsteps of those who've forsaken earthly riches, bear witness to a life of rigorous simplicity. Their fare, meager and sparing, sustains them not for indulgence but for the holy work that doth lay before them. Hours are spent in the solitude of contemplation or in the fervent study of sacred texts, seeking illumination in the divine word. Yet, not all moments are claimed by solitude; for the community gathers in earnest for daily chores, each task however humble, performed in a spirit of brotherly love and mutual support. Amidst these rhythms of prayer and labor, the friars venture forth into the world, their words sowing seeds of faith amongst the people, a testament to their boundless devotion. In this manner, day yields to night, and the friars retire once more to their modest quarters, their hearts and minds lifted heavenward, a reflection of their unyielding commitment to a life consecrated to the service of the Almighty.

Prayers, Preaching, and Community Within the cloistered walls and beyond, the very essence of the daily life of a friar dwells amidst prayers, preaching, and a profound sense of community. Thomas Aquinas, whose intellect soared to the highest contemplations of divine truths, found his earthly anchor in these humble practices. Each day dawned not just with the sun's rays but with the divine light of morning prayers, illuminating the path of those devoted to a life of poverty, chastity, and obedience.

In the hallowed hours of the morning, the monastery echoed with the collective voices of brethren joined in prayer. This was not merely a ritual but the foundation of their spiritual fortitude. For Aquinas, prayer was the compass that directed his scholarly pursuits, ensuring his works were always in service to the Greater Glory. In the tranquil silence that followed communal prayers, he found the clarity and inspiration that fueled his theological inquiries.

Yet, Aquinas knew that faith without works was an unlit candle. Thus, preaching became the extension of his prayer, a means to spread the divine wisdom he sought to understand. Walking the line between the scholarly and the divine, his sermons reached out to the hearts of the learned and the lay alike. His elegant oratory wove complex theological concepts into comprehensible truths, making the divine accessible to all.

The sense of community within the monastery was palpable. It transcended mere cohabitation; it was a divine bond forged in shared faith and service. Aquinas, despite his towering intellect, stood as a brother among brothers. His humility was a testament to his belief in the equality of all men under God. It was in this brotherhood that Aquinas found both solace and strength, a refuge from the rigors of intellectual pursuits.

The monastic schedule, divided between labor, study, and prayer, was a rhythmic dance to the tune of divine service. Aquinas, in his devotion, embraced this rhythm, finding joy in the simplicity of monastic duties. His participation in the daily tasks of the monastery served as a reminder of the joy found in service and the value of communal living.

Feasts and fasts marked the passage of time, each observance a thread woven into the fabric of their spiritual life. Aquinas approached these periods with reverence, understanding them as opportunities for spiritual growth and renewal. Through fasting, he practiced self-denial, a physical testament to his inner dedication to God. The feasts, meanwhile, were celebrations of divine generosity, reminders of the spiritual bounty that sustains the soul.

In the quiet moments of personal prayer, Aquinas delved into the depths of his soul, seeking communion with the Divine. These moments of solitude were not born out of a desire for isolation but a pursuit of deeper understanding and intimacy with God. It was here, in the silence of his heart, that Aquinas encountered the profound mysteries of faith.

The infirmary offered another dimension to the communal life, a place where the physical frailties of man met with the compassion of Christ. Aquinas, tending to the sick, embodied the loving hands of Christ. His care for his brethren in their time of need spoke volumes of his character, illuminating his understanding of Christ's teachings on love and service.

Evenings brought the community back together in prayer, a time to reflect on the day's work and seek guidance for the morrow. For Aquinas, this was a time of gratitude, an opportunity to give thanks for the day's blessings and the strength to overcome its trials. The Vespers echoed the community's united voice, a chorus of faith ascending to the heavens.

The sharing of meals was more than a physical necessity; it was a sacred act of fellowship. Aquinas, breaking bread with his brethren, found joy in the simplicity of communal eating. These moments, shared in contemplation and conversation, reinforced the bonds of brotherhood.

Guidance and correction, provided with compassion and understanding, ensured the spiritual growth of the community. Aquinas, in his wisdom, offered counsel to his brethren, guiding them in their spiritual journey. His advice, steeped in humility and love, fostered an environment of mutual respect and growth.

The celebration of the Eucharist stood as the pinnacle of their communal life, a moment of profound unity with Christ and one another. Aquinas, partaking in the body and blood of Christ, experienced the ultimate communion, a foretaste of the heavenly banquet. It was this sacramental union that fueled his theological pursuits, a constant reminder of the divine mysteries he sought to comprehend.

Seasons changed, but the rhythm of prayer, preaching, and community remained, each day a testament to their dedication to God. Aquinas's life within this rhythm was a beautiful harmony of faith and reason, a living illustration of the theology he espoused.

As the years passed, the impact of Aquinas's life and works echoed beyond the monastery walls. Yet, at the heart of his legacy was the simple, profound life he led among his brethren. In prayers, preaching, and community, Aquinas found the true essence of divine service, a mirror reflecting the love of Christ.

In sum, the life of Thomas Aquinas, marked by the sanctity of prayers, the wisdom of preaching, and the warmth of community, stands as a beacon to all who seek to unite intellect and faith. His journey, grounded in the humble practices of monastic life, reveals the path to true enlightenment: a life lived in unwavering service to God and man.

Chapter 6: Battles Against Heresy

In an age where the pestilence of heresy did spread its vile root deep within Christendom's very heart, Thomas Aquinas standeth as a bastion of Orthodoxy, wielding not but his faith and intellect in the grand struggle. Within the annals of this chapter, we unveil the theatrics of Aquinas's fervent crusade against the doctrines that sought to undermine the very foundation upon which the Church did firmly stand. 'Twas a time most fraught with peril, as the tendrils of Albigensianism, with its scorn for the material world, did seek to beguile the souls of men towards paths divergent from the Holy Writ. Yet, fear not, for Aquinas, armed with wisdom and the spirit of divine grace, entered the arena of public discourse, his voice a clarion call that echoed through the chambers of learning and the halls of power alike.

His battles were not wrought with sword and shield, but with the mightier implements of dialogue and treatise. Peerless he was in the art of disputation, tackling the manifold heresies with a mind as sharp as a two-edged sword, and a heart inflamed with the love of Christ. It was through these public debates, engaging with adversarial ideas head-on, that Aquinas proved himself not merely a luminary in scholastic theology, but a stalwart defender of the faith. Each argument laid bare, each heretical notion dismantled with precision, served as testament to his unyielding commitment to the pursuit of truth and the propagation of the gospel. So, let us venture forth into the thick of these battles against heresy, witnessing how Aquinas's indomitable spirit and unwavering faith wielded the power of persuasion and reason not as mere tools of rhetoric, but as divine instruments of salvation.

The Fight for Orthodoxy

In the midst of tumult and doctrinal uproar, Thomas Aquinas stood as a bulwark against the encroaching tide of heresy that sought to undermine the Church's teachings. The stage was set for a confrontation that would echo through the annals of history, a veritable clash of titans beneath the scrutinizing gaze of Heaven. Aquinas, armed with naught but his wit and an unwavering faith in the Almighty, did boldly step into the fray, challenging those who dared to distort the teachings of Christ for their own ends. His encounters, fraught with peril, were not merely battles of words but of souls, wherein the very essence of Christian orthodoxy was at stake. Each debate, each disputation, served as a testament to his profound understanding of divine truth and his unrelenting commitment to safeguard it against perversion. Through public debates and rigorous challenges, Aquinas did not merely defend the orthodoxy; he illuminated its truths, compelling friend and foe alike to acknowledge the supreme authority of the Church's teachings. This chapter of his life reveals not only the steadfastness of his character but also the depth of his devotion, proving that knowledge, when wielded with faith, can indeed serve as a mighty servant to orthodoxy.

Public Debates and Challenges

In the annals of history, few have stood so fervently in defense of orthodoxy as Thomas Aquinas. His encounters in the public sphere, marked by debates and challenges, are a testament to his unwavering faith and intellectual prowess. The stage was oft set in places of learning or ecclesiastical power where minds keen and sharp as swords clashed over matters of doctrine and belief.

It was not uncommon for Thomas to find himself amidst the throngs of dissenters, those who, drawn by currents of heresy, sought to undermine the very foundations of the Church. Yet, with a heart emboldened by divine grace and a mind sharpened by years of studious labor, Aquinas engaged his adversaries with a calmness that belied the intensity of his spirit.

The public debates in which Aquinas partook were far from mere intellectual exercises; they were battles for the soul of Christendom. Heretics, armed with twisted interpretations of scripture and philosophy, endeavored to sway the uncertain and to fortify the ranks of the misguided. Aquinas, recognizing the peril these false prophets posed, did set forth to confront them, not with sword and shield, but with the mightier tools of reason and faith.

His method was one of meticulous clarity and unwavering patience. Aquinas would first listen, truly listen, to the arguments presented by his opponents. He sought not just to refute but to understand, to find the root of their error and, in doing so, guide them back to truth. This approach, revolutionary in its application, served to disarm many a rival, leaving them more susceptible to the light of reason.

Among the many challenges Aquinas faced, none were more daunting than those posed by the radical interpretations of Aristotelian philosophy. In an age where Aristotle's works were rediscovered and gaining prominence, many attempted to reconcile his teachings with Christian doctrine, often straying into heretical territory. Aquinas, with his profound understanding of both Aristotle and Church teachings, adeptly navigated these treacherous waters, presenting arguments that illuminated the harmony between faith and reason.

The resilience of Aquinas was put to the test in Paris, where the atmosphere of intellectual rivalry was most palpable. Here, scholars of varying allegiances engaged in verbal duels, each seeking to assert the superiority of their views. Thomas, in his humility, did not shy away from these confrontations but welcomed them as opportunities to defend the truth. His performances in these settings solidified his reputation as a formidable theologian and philosopher.

One cannot speak of Thomas Aquinas's public challenges without mentioning his encounters with the Albigensians. This sect, with their dualistic worldview and rejection of material reality as inherently evil, stood in stark opposition to the teachings of the Church. Aquinas, understanding the danger they posed to the faithful, took it upon himself to counter their claims, using not only scripture and tradition but also logic and natural law to dismantle their arguments.

Moreover, Thomas's commitment to orthodoxy was not limited to verbal disputes. He was prolific in his written works, many of which served as direct responses to the heresies of his time. His "Summa Contra Gentiles" and "Summa Theologica" are crowning achievements in this regard, offering comprehensive rebuttals to the errors that plagued the Church. These texts, while scholastic in nature, were born from the challenges Aquinas faced in the public arena.

Aquinas's debates were not mere spectacles of intellectual prowess; they were acts of service to the Church and to God. Every argument refuted, every heresy debunked, was a victory for the truth. His ability to engage with and persuade those of differing beliefs was not just a testament to his brilliance but to his profound love for God and His creation.

The legacy of Thomas Aquinas in the realm of public debates and challenges endures to this day. His approach to engaging with opponents, grounded in respect, understanding, and an unwavering commitment to truth, serves as a beacon for all who seek to navigate the treacherous waters of theological and philosophical discourse.

In reflecting upon the life and works of Aquinas, one cannot help but be inspired by his dedication to the defense of faith through reason. It is a reminder that the pursuit of truth is not for the faint of heart. It requires courage, integrity, and an unwavering trust in the power of divine wisdom.

Thus, the story of Thomas Aquinas's public debates and challenges is not just a historical account of theological disputes; it is a testament to the enduring power of faith guided by reason. In a world fraught with confusion and error, the legacy of Aquinas shines as a guiding light, showing the path to enlightenment and truth.

In sum, Aquinas's public endeavors highlight a profound conviction: that knowledge serves faith, and that reason, when coupled with divine grace, holds the key to understanding both the mysteries of creation and the heart of the Creator. For those who tread the path of inquiry and belief, Aquinas's life stands as a monument to the triumph of faith informed by reason, beckoning to all who seek to reconcile the divine with the human.

Therefore, let us take heed of Aquinas's example, daring to engage with the world not as adversaries but as instruments of God's truth. For in the challenges we face, we find not obstacles but opportunities to affirm our faith, to refine our reason, and to draw ever closer to the divine. Verily, the trials of yesterday pave the way for the triumphs of tomorrow, and in the figure of Thomas Aquinas, we find both a champion of orthodoxy and a herald of hope for the ages.

Confronting the Albigensians

In an epoch where darkness sought to obscure the light of orthodoxy, the Albigensian heresy spread like a pestilence through the heart of Christendom, challenging the very foundation upon which the Church stood. This grievous error, veiling itself under the guise of piety, did verily propagate doctrines most contrary to the Holy Scripture. It was in this tumultuous time that the Church, as a steadfast guardian of the faith, did call upon its most devout and erudite champions to defend the besieged truth. Among these valiant defenders was none other than Thomas Aquinas, whose intellect was as a beacon shining forth amidst the tempest, illuminating the path to salvation for those led astray by the Albigensian deception.

With the word of God as his sword and reason as his shield, Aquinas ventured into the heart of the conflict, engaging in disputation with a zeal borne of divine inspiration. His arguments, grounded in the teachings of Scripture and the natural law, did reveal the Albigensian doctrine as a chimerical fantasy, devoid of the light of truth. Through his tireless efforts, many who had been ensnared by the Albigensian lies were brought back into the fold of the Church, their faith restored and their souls safeguarded from eternal damnation. Thus did Aquinas, by the grace of God and the strength of his conviction, confront the Albigensians, demonstrating that knowledge, when wedded to faith, is the most potent weapon against the forces of heresy.

The Power of Persuasion and Faith As we wade deeper into the heart of our discourse, let us turn our gaze to the profound skirmish waged 'gainst the tide of Albigensian heresy. Pitted are not merely beliefs in stark contrast but the very souls of men, whose salvation hangs in the balance. The stage is set, and our champion, Thomas Aquinas, armed with naught but the power of persuasion and undying faith, steps forth into the arena.

It was in the era when shadows of uncertainty crept upon the faithful, casting doubt where light once reigned. The Albigensians, with teachings most contrary to the Church's heart, sowed seeds of discord amongst the people. Their doctrine, shrouded in a cloak of spiritual elitism, dismissed the material world as an inherently evil creation, anathema to the loving Creator professed by the Church.

Aquinas, whose life was a testament to the harmonious blend of faith and reason, could not stand idly by as the faithful were led astray. With the might of his intellect and the depth of his spiritual conviction, he embarked upon a crusade not of swords and fire but of words and enlightenment. For he knew well that the fiercest battles for the Lord are often fought in the hearts and minds of His people.

His first assault against the heresy was not borne of condemnation but understanding. Aquinas delved deep into the heart of Albigensian beliefs, engaging in dialogue with its adherents. His approach was not to alienate but to draw them nearer, using the power of gentle persuasion to unveil the inconsistencies of their doctrine.

Through debate and discussion, Aquinas showcased the beauty of the Church's teachings, illustrating the world not as a prison of flesh but as a creation born of divine love. The material world, he argued, was imbued with the Creator's grace, where each creature, each plant, and every man could lead one closer to understanding God's nature.

Yet, his words were not merely empty rhetoric. Aquinas fortified his arguments with the bedrock of scripture and the teachings of the Church Fathers. Each point he made was a thread in a larger tapestry, weaving together faith and reason into a compelling narrative that appealed to both the heart and the intellect.

As his debates with the Albigensians continued, it became clear that Aquinas's mastery of persuasion was not solely of human design. Each word, each sentence, seemed to carry with it the whisper of the Divine, touching the hearts of those who had long been ensnared by heretical thought.

In this great endeavor, Aquinas's faith was his shield and his love for the truth his sword. It was evident to all who witnessed his passionate defense of the faith that his strength stemmed not from pride or the desire for victory, but from a humble submission to God's will.

His encounters with the Albigensians were not merely debates but acts of faith. Aquinas's unwavering belief in the goodness of God's creation and the redemptive power of Christ's love shone through his every word, becoming a beacon of hope for those trapped in spiritual darkness.

Through his persistent efforts, the tide began to turn. Hearts once hardened by the Albigensian doctrine opened to the message of salvation through Christ. Communities that had been torn asunder by heretical beliefs found healing in the Church's teachings, rekindled by Aquinas's persuasive eloquence.

What Aquinas's story teaches us is the transcendent power of faith when wielded with love and understanding. It was not through coercion or force that he engaged the Albigensians but with a heart open to dialogue and a mind sharp with the wisdom of the Church's teachings.

In our modern age, where voices of dissent and disbelief are many, the lessons of Aquinas's encounters with the Albigensians remain profoundly relevant. The path to enlightenment and salvation, as he so eloquently demonstrated, is paved with the stones of reason, faith, and an unwavering commitment to the truth.

Thus, let us take from Aquinas not just the might of his intellect but the depth of his faith and the wisdom of his approach. For in our journey to bring light to those who walk in darkness, it is the power of persuasion and faith, guided by love, that will illuminate the path.

So it stands, a testament not merely to the brilliance of Aquinas's mind but to the indomitable spirit of his faith. The battle against the Albigensian heresy was not won by force but by the compelling power of truth, a truth that resonates through the ages, calling all to the embrace of the Church's teachings.

In closing, let us not forget the essence of Aquinas's triumph. It is a beacon of hope that faith, when paired with reason and articulated with love, holds the power to overcome even the darkest of heresies. May we all be so inspired to wield these tools with the grace and conviction of Thomas Aquinas, for the glory of God and the salvation of souls. Amen.

Chapter 7: Masterworks of Theology

In the annals of faith and reason, none shine so bright as the masterworks sprung from the mind of Thomas Aquinas. The jewel in this crown of theological achievement, the *Summa Theologica*, stands as a monument to the symbiosis of divine truth and human inquiry. Crafted with the precision of a scholar and the passion of a believer, this titanic text sought not merely to catalogue the mysteries of the divine but to make them accessible to the minds of men. Within its pages, Aquinas unfurls the tapestry of Christian doctrine, each question and article a thread woven with the care of a theologian deeply in love with both God and logic.

Yet, 'twas not solely in the *Summa* that Aquinas's brilliance was manifest. His corpus extends into realms vast with commentaries on Scripture, Aristotle, and topics as varied as the nature of angels and the morality of war. These other significant contributions, though they may dwell in the shadow of the *Summa Theologica*, are no less vital. Through lectures, opuscula, and exegeses, Aquinas rendered the abstract concrete, the divine intimate, and the complex comprehensible, ever serving both faith and reason in a harmonious embrace.

Each work, each word penned by Aquinas, serves as a beacon for those traversing the foggy realms of doubt and disbelief. By arguments robust and convictions unwavering, he invites all to see beyond the veil of the material, to the sublime truths that dance just beyond the reach of reason alone. In plumbing the depths of theology, Aquinas has charted a course not just for scholars and theologians, but for any soul daring to quest for truth in the vast sea of existence. Thus, his masterworks endure, not merely as relics of a bygone age, but as living texts, calling each reader to embark on their own journey toward enlightenment.

The Summa Theologica

Within the annals of theology, the magnus opus of St. Thomas Aquinas, *The Summa Theologica,* Towers as a veritable colossus, casting its long shadow o'er the realm of scholastic argumentation and devout inquiry. Designed with an architect's precision and a poet's grace, this masterwork sought nought but to lay bare the very foundation upon which faith and reason harmoniously intertwine. Through its quintessential structure - the Question, followed by Objection, and culminated with Resolution - Aquinas doth guide the inquisitive soul on a pilgrimage from the depths of doubt to the pinnacle of celestial understanding. 'Tis a testament not merely to the brilliance of Aquinas's intellect but to his unwavering belief in the sanctity of questioning as the pathway to divine truth. Each page of this seminal tome serves not only as an argument but as an invocation, urging believers and skeptics alike to behold the majesty of creation, and therein, find the immutable evidence of the Creator. So crafted, *The Summa Theologica* stands not merely as an academic endeavor but as a beacon, illuminating the path from empirical evidence to spiritual enlightenment, proving, beyond the shadow of a doubt, that knowledge serves at the behest of faith, leading unerringly to the recognition of Jesus as the Son of God.

Design and Purpose In the grand tapestry of Christian scholarship, the work of Thomas Aquinas stands as a towering monument, a beacon of intellectual rigour and divine inspiration. Within the voluminous expanse of his writings, the Summa Theologica emerges as the quintessence of his life's endeavour. Crafted with the meticulous precision of a master artisan, its purpose transcends the mere compilation of theological knowledge; rather, it endeavors to lay bare the foundational truths of existence and the divine, offering a map to navigate the complex interplay of faith and reason.

When one delves into the Summa, it becomes evident that Aquinas's intent was not solely to educate but to transform. Each question and article within it is designed not as an isolated nugget of wisdom but as a stepping stone towards a greater understanding of the divine mysteries. Aquinas, with a sage's foresight, recognized the perils of unbelief and skepticism that lay in wait for souls untutored in the ways of faith. His response, through this monumental work, was to fortify the intellect with the armour of reason and the shield of faith.

The Summa's design is a thing of beauty, a labyrinthine structure that invites exploration. Its division into three main parts speaks to a holistic vision of humanity's relationship with God: from the foundational principles of being and the essence of God, through the moral and ethical pathways for human conduct, to the culmination in Christ and the Sacraments which bridge the finite and the infinite. Aquinas masterfully interweaves Aristotelian philosophy with Christian doctrine, demonstrating that truth, whether revealed or discovered through reason, flows from the same Divine source.

In architecting the Summa, Aquinas illuminated the path for countless souls seeking understanding and clarity in matters of faith. The purpose guiding his quill was none other than to elucidate the harmonious coherence between reason and revelation. By demonstrating how natural reason supports and uplifts faith, Aquinas extended an olive branch to the skeptics of his time, inviting them into a dialogue grounded in mutual respect for truth.

Moreover, the Summa serves as a testament to Aquinas's humility and his unshakeable belief in the supremacy of divine wisdom. In its pages, one finds not the voice of a man seeking personal glory but the humble servant of God, striving to unveil the splendour of the Creator's grand design. Aquinas, in his unwavering commitment to this task, becomes a mirror reflecting the divine light, guiding others to the source of all truth.

The methodical approach adopted by Aquinas, characterized by the posing of a question, the presentation of objections, and then a reasoned response, fosters a dynamic engagement with the text. This dialectical method encourages readers to actively grapple with the ideas presented, ensuring that the journey through the Summa is not a passive reception of wisdom but an active cultivation of understanding.

Furthermore, the Summa's purpose extends beyond the academic to the profoundly spiritual. Aquinas did not conceive it merely as an intellectual exercise; rather, he envisioned it as a ladder to the divine, a means by which souls might ascend to greater heights of spiritual realization. Through the rigorous application of reason, readers are invited to deepen their relationship with God, to move beyond the superficialities of faith to its most profound depths.

The design of the Summa, with its meticulous organization and systematic approach, embodies Aquinas's conviction in the orderly nature of the universe and the rationality underpinning divine law. In reflecting this divine order, the Summa itself becomes a vehicle through which the mind is raised to the contemplation of God. It stands as a beacon of hope, affirming that truth is accessible, that faith and reason are not in conflict but are complementary pathways to the same ultimate reality: God.

In crafting the Summa Theologica, Aquinas provided a repository of wisdom that has nourished the souls of believers and seekers of truth across centuries. Its enduring relevance lies in its capacity to address the fundamental questions of existence, ethics, and the divine with clarity, depth, and an unwavering commitment to truth. The Summa remains a vital resource for those navigating the tumultuous seas of doubt and belief, offering a sure anchor in the unchanging truths of Christian doctrine.

The magnificence of the Summa's design and the nobility of its purpose underscore Aquinas's extraordinary contribution to Christian theology and Western thought. It encapsulates his philosophical and theological genius, his dedication to the pursuit of truth, and his heartfelt desire to guide others towards the light of Christ. In the Summa Theologica, Aquinas has bequeathed to humanity a masterpiece that continues to inspire, enlighten, and draw souls closer to God.

The Summa, therefore, stands not merely as a work of theology but as a beacon of hope and a guide for the perplexed. It calls out through the ages to all those who seek truth, offering answers grounded in reason and faith. Aquinas's masterwork remains a testament to the power of the human intellect when humbly submitted to the service of faith, a reminder that knowledge is but the servant of the divine.

In the grand design and noble purpose of the Summa Theologica, one discerns the heart of Thomas Aquinas himself: a heart aflame with love for God and an unwavering commitment to the truth. It is a work that beckons not just to the mind but to the soul, inviting all who encounter it to embark on a journey of intellectual and spiritual discovery that leads, ultimately, to God.

Thus, in the end, the Summa Theologica serves as a bridge between heaven and earth, an invitation to explore the depths of divine wisdom. Through its pages, Aquinas extends to us all a call to embark on the greatest adventure of all: the quest to know and love God more deeply. In embracing this call, we find not only the answers to our deepest questions but the fulfillment of our ultimate purpose.

Therefore, in the Summa Theologica, we are presented with not just a work of theological brilliance but a beacon of spiritual guidance. Its design and purpose reflect the very essence of Aquinas's mission: to illuminate the path to God through the rigor of reason and the luminescence of faith. In this, Aquinas remains an ever-relevant guide, a teacher for the ages, beckoning us ever onwards towards enlightenment and salvation through Jesus Christ.

Other Significant Contributions

Among the vast sea of scholastic achievement, where the works of Thomas Aquinas gleam like stars in the firmament of theology, there lie hidden treasures yet to be fully explored by the minds keen on discerning the divine. Within the hallowed pages of his commentaries, opuscula, and lectures, one finds the whisperings of eternal truths, delicately interwoven with the rigorous intellect of scholarly pursuit. These texts serve not as mere footnotes in the grand narrative of Thomistic thought but as pillars upon which the mighty edifice of his theology stands. Each commentary, whether upon the sacred scriptures or the philosophies of the ancients, reveals the depth of Aquinas's insight, proving his mastery over both faith and reason. The opuscula, those shorter treatises on matters of profound spiritual and ethical import, further unveil the breadth of Aquinas's vision, demonstrating his unwavering commitment to the elucidation of truth. The lectures, delivered with the passion of one who is both teacher and seeker, echo through the centuries as a testament to the enduring power of Aquinas's intellect and spirit. In these less celebrated works, scholars, theologians, and students alike may yet find fresh inspiration and new pathways to understanding, for within them lies the heart of a man who knew no greater love than the pursuit of wisdom in the service of the Almighty.

Commentaries, Opuscula, and Lectures Amidst the vast sea of Aquinas's scholarly endeavors, one finds the treasure of his commentaries, opuscula, and lectures. These works, arguably as monumental in their own rite as his more frequently cited Masterworks, provide a window into the very soul of Aquinas's theological and philosophical journey. They serve not merely as texts, but as beacons guiding the faithful towards an understanding divine beyond the grasp of mere mortals.

In these lesser showcased pieces, Aquinas engaged with a variety of texts, ranging from the sacred scriptures to the ponderings of Aristotle. His commentaries, with meticulous care and insatiable curiosity, sought to unravel the complexities of existence and divine law. It was here that Aquinas's genius shone bright, as he charted pathways through the dense forests of thought that had bewildered many a mind before him.

The opuscula, those smaller works attributed to Aquinas, were no less significant in their impact. Though they may not boast the grandeur of his Summa Theologica, within their brevity they encapsulate the essence of Aquinas's theological endeavor. They were akin to the sparks from a blacksmith's forge, each capable of igniting fires of faith and reason across generations.

Aquinas's lectures, meanwhile, offered a more personal glimpse into the scholar's mind. They were the medium through which he conversed with the minds of the future, imparting wisdom in a manner that transcended the confines of time and space. Through them, one can hear the echoes of Aquinas's voice, a voice that endeavored to reconcile the world to its Creator.

What is often overlooked in the pursuit of grasping Aquinas's intellect is the profound humility with which he approached his subject matter. In his commentaries, there resounds a tone of deference to the wisdom of ages past. Aquinas positioned himself not as a master inventing anew but as a diligent student, piecing together the mosaic of divine revelation.

His method in dissecting Aristotle's texts, for instance, revealed a disposition of both reverence and critical engagement. It was a delicate dance of faith and reason, where Aquinas led his readers through the complex choreographies of thought, always with the assurance of faith's primacy.

The import of Aquinas's lectures cannot be overstated. In these gatherings, his words were not mere theoretical musings but were charged with the urgency of a soul in pursuit of Truth. His audience, composed of fellow seekers, was invited to partake in this sacred quest, guided by Aquinas's unwavering conviction in the light of faith.

Among the opuscula, certain texts stand out for their profound exploration of specific theological and philosophical quandaries. These works, though small in size, are colossal in their theological and philosophical implications. They delve into matters such as the nature of evil, the virtues, and the beatitudes, offering insights that are at once piercing and edifying.

The accessibility of Aquinas's lectures and opuscula speaks volumes of his intention. It was not to tower solitary in the realm of thought but to extend a hand to those who might wish to climb alongside him. His works are not simply to be admired but engaged with, wrestled with, and ultimately, lived.

Through his commentaries, Aquinas bridged worlds. He brought the ethereal into conversation with the terrestrial, urging a harmonious discourse between faith and reason. In these texts, one observes Aquinas the philosopher and theologian not in conflict but in beautiful synthesis.

This synthesis is perhaps most evident in his Biblical commentaries. Here, the scriptures were not merely texts to be dissected but were the living word, prompting an encounter with the divine. Aquinas approached these sacred texts with both the intellect of a scholar and the heart of a believer, demonstrating that faith and understanding are not mutually exclusive but mutually enriching.

The enduring relevance of these works lies in their capacity to speak to the contemporary soul. In a world often fragmented by dichotomies, Aquinas's commentaries, opuscula, and lectures remind us of the possibility of a synthesis that transcends division. They beckon the modern mind to a higher pursuit, where the quest for knowledge is anchored in the quest for the divine.

In conclusion, the corpus of Aquinas's commentaries, opuscula, and lectures stands as a testament to his intellectual and spiritual legacy. They encapsulate a journey of a mind and soul in unceasing pursuit of truth. For the faithful, they offer a wellspring of wisdom; for the skeptic, a challenge to deeper inquiry; and for all, an invitation to partake in the eternal dialogue between faith and reason.

Thus, to delve into these works is to walk in the footsteps of Aquinas himself, tracing the contours of a life devoted to the highest ideals of scholarship and sanctity. In them, we find not only the brilliance of Aquinas's mind but the radiance of his faith, illuminating the path towards the divine, where knowledge serves as the handmaiden of faith.

Let us, therefore, embrace the legacy of Aquinas's commentaries, opuscula, and lectures with the same fervor with which they were penned. May they inspire in us a renewed zeal for truth, guiding us ever closer to the heart of the divine mystery that Aquinas so ardently sought to comprehend.

Chapter 8: Trials and Tribulations

In the midst of his fervent endeavors to unfold the divine mysteries through the lantern of reason, Thomas Aquinas was beset by manifold trials and tribulations, both of the spirit and the flesh. An accusation of heresy, that vile slander, was thrust upon him; yet, like a steadfast ship amidst tempestuous waves, he did maintain the course of orthodoxy, defending the truth of the Holy Church with a vigor that could only be kindled by a heart aflame with the love of God. 'Twas not only in the realm of contentious discourse that Aquinas found himself beleaguered. The ceaseless toil over sacred texts and the relentless pursuit of wisdom exacted a grievous toll upon his mortal frame. Ailments manifold besieged him, yet, verily, these physical afflictions served but to temper his spirit, much as the finest steel is forged in the fiercest flame. As a scholar, he laid upon himself the sacrifice of ceaseless labor, offering up his pains and sufferings as a testament to his devotion to the divine truth. Thus, in the very midst of these trials and tribulations, Thomas Aquinas did shine forth as a beacon of faith, demonstrating to all that the path to God's light is oft paved with hardship and adversity, yet it is this very journey through the shadows that renders the destination all the more glorious.

Accusations of Heresy

In a time when orthodoxy was the bulwark against the tumults of heretical fervor, our protagonist, Thomas Aquinas, found himself ensnared in a web of accusation most foul. Like unto Daniel in the den of lions, he stood unblemished by the venomous whispers that sought to tarnish his dedication to the faith. It came to pass that certain factions, envious of his intellect and suspicious of his methods, dared to assail his works as contrary to the teachings of the Church. With ardor and erudition, Thomas faced these calumnies as only a man of his stature could. Armed with reason as his shield and faith as his lance, he met his detractors in the lists of theological debate. It was not merely a defense of his own reputation that he mounted, but a stalwart defense of the orthodoxy he cherished.

Defense of Orthodoxy As we traverse yon history of our beloved Church, 'tis not without noting that the bucolic meadows of faith were oft marred by the thistles of heresy. Amongst those who wielded the scythe to cut down these weeds, none was more steadfast and valiant than Thomas Aquinas, whose mind was as a fortress unbreached, protecting the orthodoxy of Christendom with both intelligence and divine grace. His journey, marked by trials and tribulations, situates him as a towering figure in the annals of ecclesiastical defense.

In an age when shadows of doubt crept upon the hearts of men, it was Aquinas who, like a Pharos against the night, offered illumination through reason and faith intertwined. His ability to discourse theologically, whilst engaging with the philosophies of Aristotle, adorned the teachings of the Church with a robustness hitherto unseen. Not merely content to reaffirm what was believed, he ventured further, presenting a cogent defense that the orthodoxy of the Church was not only a bastion of spiritual truth but also the most rational elucidation of the divine.

His encounters with accusations of heresy were not of a tempestuous kind, filled with wrath or disdain for his accusers. Nay, Aquinas approached such confrontations with a mien of calm and respect, understanding perhaps that those who strayed were themselves seeking illumination but wandered astray. His method: to engage, not enrage; to elucidate, not obfuscate; thus bringing those ensnared in heresy closer to the light of truth through reason and patient dialogue.

The very essence of his defense lay in the Summa Theologica, a monumental work that sought to address every conceivable query about God, existence, and morality. Every question posed was an opportunity for Aquinas to weave together a tapestry of logical argumentation and scriptural truth, demonstrating that true faith was not contrary to reason but was its completest fulfillment.

Within the hallowed halls of Paris, where minds as bright as the stars above converged, Aquinas's teachings faced rigorous scrutiny. Yet, like gold tested in fire, his defense of orthodoxy emerged purer, stronger, convincing both skeptics and believers of the soundness of Church doctrine. His efforts were not merely for the academics in their ivory towers but served to guide the common believer, grounding their faith in the bedrock of reason and divine revelation.

One must not err, however, in visualizing Aquinas's journey as devoid of personal cost. The defense of orthodoxy demanded of him not only intellectual rigor but a profound spiritual resilience. The accusations, the debates, the sheer toil of writing – all exacted their toll, yet his resolve wavered not. For he saw in each challenge not a burden, but a divine calling to affirm the truth of Christ's teachings amidst the tempests of doubt.

In combating the Albigensian heresy, Aquinas did not wield the sword nor the flame, but the mightier power of his intellect and faith. The Albigensians, with their dualistic worldview, presented a stark challenge to the Church's teachings. Yet, Aquinas, through careful argumentation and a deep compassion for the souls of the misled, sought to dispel the darkness of their beliefs with the light of orthodoxy. His writings against such heresies were not merely polemics but heartfelt attempts to guide the lost sheep back to the fold.

Indeed, his life's work may be seen as a continuous dialogue with those both within and without the Church's sanctuary. Each question posed, each doubt raised, he met with an unwavering commitment to truth, always maintaining that at the heart of the Church's teachings lay the path to ultimate reality and salvation.

The efficacy of Aquinas's defense was not borne merely of his intellectual prowess but also his saintly character. His contemporaries and those who followed bore witness to a man whose life was a testament to the truths he defended. In his humility, his devotion, and his tireless labor, Aquinas embodied the orthodoxy he so ardently championed.

Thus, in the fullness of time, the Church, recognizing the indelible mark Aquinas had left upon the defense of her teachings, sought to honor him with the title of Doctor of the Church. This was not merely an accolade but a recognition of his role as a guardian of orthodoxy, a title bestowed upon those whose work and witness have been deemed of profound significance for the faith.

Yet, let us not be swayed into believing that his influence rests solely in the annals of history. The defense of orthodoxy, as articulated by Aquinas, continues to resonate, offering guidance and clarity in an age still fraught with challenges to the faith. His works serve as beacons, guiding the Church as she navigates the tumultuous waters of modernity, proving that the truths he defended are not bound by time but are eternal.

In conclusion, the Defense of Orthodoxy by Thomas Aquinas stands as a monumental testament to the synthesis of faith and reason. In his tireless effort to protect and elucidate the teachings of the Church, he demonstrated that the true essence of orthodoxy is not rigidity but the unyielding pursuit of truth, guided by the light of reason and the divine inspiration of faith. His legacy, thus, is not merely in the texts he left behind but in the enduring strength of the Church's teachings, fortified by his intellect, his faith, and his profound devotion to the truth of the Gospel.

Therefore, in reflecting upon the life and work of Aquinas, let us be inspired by his unwavering defense of orthodoxy. May we, in our various vocations, be so moved by the Holy Spirit to defend the faith with equal parts reason and reverence, ensuring that the light of truth, so brilliantly articulated by Aquinas, continues to shine forth in a world ever in need of its guiding brilliance.

Physical Ailments and the Toll of Toil

In the chapter of his earthly pilgrimage named *Trials and Tribulations*, one must ponder the afflictions and hardships that our stalwart Aquinas endured. Verily, the body is but a vessel, yet how ponderous the toll when the spirit's endeavor doth weigh upon flesh and bone! His relentless pursuit of divine wisdom, fueled by an unquenchable thirst for understanding the mysteries of the Divine, exacted a grievous toll upon his health. Hours upon end, cloistered within the dim confines of his cell or bent over ancient texts in the hallowed halls of learning, Aquinas's labor was ceaseless. His visage, oft illuminated by the flicker of candlelight, bore the marks of his toil; eyes strained and body weary from his endless devotion to study and prayer. **Forsooth**, it was not merely the scourge of physical ailment that beset him, but the profound weariness of soul that accompanies such singular dedication to a cause greater than oneself. This tale of sacrifice speaks to us across the ages, reminding us that the quest for truth and enlightenment, whilst noble, demands its pound of flesh, and serves as a testament to the indomitable spirit that carried Aquinas through his terrestrial journey.

A Scholar's Sacrifice In the ensuing chapters, we have traversed the life and intellectual odyssey of Thomas Aquinas, whose contributions have indeed left an indelible mark upon the realms of theology and philosophy. Yet, his journey was not without its profound sacrifices, a testament to the cost of greatness and the pursuit of divine truth.

The chronicles of Aquinas' life reveal a man utterly devoted to the elucidation and propagation of theological understanding, often at the expense of his physical health and personal comforts. His decision to embrace a life of mendicancy, renouncing worldly riches for spiritual wealth, was but the first step in a series of sacrifices that would define his existence.

Aquinas' daily regimen was nothing short of austere. Rising before dawn, his hours were consumed by prayer, study, and the composition of scholarly works that sought to bridge the chasm between faith and reason. The magnitude of his intellectual endeavors was such that he often forwent the basic necessities of rest and nourishment.

Upon reflection, one marvels at the sheer volume of his compositions, notably the *Summa Theologica*, which remains a cornerstone of Catholic doctrine. The laborious process of handwriting each manuscript, in an era devoid of printing technology, underscores the physical toll exacted upon Aquinas.

Moreover, his unyielding commitment to academic integrity and orthodoxy exposed him to accusations of heresy, a burden of stress that would accompany him throughout his service to the Church. These trials, coupled with his dedication to his intellectual crusades, surely weighed heavily upon his mortal frame.

Yet, it was not merely physical and mental exertion that Aquinas endured. His path was fraught with spiritual trials as well. The tale of his mystical experiences, including the divine revelations that ultimately led him to cease his writing, suggests a soul constantly wrestling with the profound mysteries of faith.

The decision to abandon his scholarly pursuits, declaring all he had written as akin to straw when compared to the glory of God's revelation, marks a poignant moment of sacrifice. It was a relinquishment of his life's work in acknowledgment of the limits of human understanding and the supremacy of divine wisdom.

This surrender, however, was not an admission of defeat but rather the ultimate declaration of faith—a demonstration that knowledge, no matter how vast, serves at the pleasure of faith. Aquinas illuminated this principle through both his life and his legacies, advocating that the pursuit of truth must ultimately lead one back to the Creator.

In his embrace of poverty, Aquinas signified his rejection of temporal power and wealth, exemplifying his belief that true riches lie in spiritual communion with God. His mendicant lifestyle was a constant reminder of his priorities, placing God above all earthly desires.

The physical ailments that accompanied his relentless scholarly efforts underscore the fragile balance between mind and body. Despite these impediments, Aquinas' resolve never wavered, his faith acting as the beacon that guided him through periods of darkness and doubt.

Engaging in public debates and confronting heresies, Aquinas not only defended the orthodoxy of his time but also paved the way for future discussions on faith and reason. These confrontations, while intellectually stimulating, were also sources of great personal strife, exposing him to public scrutiny and the ire of opponents.

Throughout these trials, Aquinas was sustained by a community of brothers and sisters in faith, whose support and understanding bolstered his spirit. The solidarity within this spiritual family was a source of strength, allowing him to persevere in his vocation.

The culmination of Aquinas' life, marked by both his mystical experiences and the cessation of his writing, invites contemplation on the nature of sacrifice in the pursuit of holiness. It stands as a beacon to those who endeavor to navigate the complex interplay between faith and reason, prompting a reflection on the sacrifices one is willing to make in the quest for divine truth.

Thus, Aquinas' life and works serve not merely as a testament to his intellect but as a clarion call to all who seek to understand the divine. In his sacrifice, we find a model of devotion, a reminder that the journey toward enlightenment is laden with trials but illuminated by the steadfast light of faith.

In closing, let us remember the sacrifices of Thomas Aquinas not as relics of a bygone era but as enduring lessons on the value of perseverance, the pursuit of truth, and the ultimate submission to divine will. Through his example, may we find the courage to make our own sacrifices in the service of faith, guided by the light of his wisdom and the grace of God.

Chapter 9: The Mystical Experiences

In the waning hours of Thomas Aquinas's Earthly pilgrimage, amidst the toil and tribulation that marked his remarkable journey, a transformative event of mystical proportions befell him. It was within this crucible of divine intimacy, when the heavens themselves did part and beheld unto him revelations ineffable. These divine illuminations imprinted upon his soul a clarity so profound, that all his prior works seemed to him as mere straw. This epiphany, a celestial whisper, compelled him to lay down his quill, declaring, "All that I have written seems like straw." The enigma of this decision perplexes to this day. For in the midst of scribing his magnum opus, why would such a towering intellect desist? Aquinas, having peered into the very essence of divinity, found his scholarly pursuits paled in comparison to the majesty and mystery of God. This narrative, illustrious as it might seem, serves not merely as an historical account but as a beckoning; a call to ponder the complexities of faith and reason. It underscores the pivotal truth that knowledge, no matter how grand, serves but as a handmaiden to faith. For in the mystical experiences of Saint Thomas Aquinas, we find a testament to the boundless mystery of the divine, inviting all, skeptic and believer alike, to marvel at the profundity of God's revelation to one of the greatest minds ever bestowed upon humanity.

Divine Revelations

In the annals of Christendom, few souls have been as mightily stirred and splendidly enlightened by divine revelation as that of Thomas Aquinas. It was upon the wings of these celestial communications that Aquinas soared beyond the mere intellect into the sublime realms of mysticism. Verily, these revelations were not of the ordinary sort, consisting of mere intangible visions or ethereal whispers. Nay, they were profound illuminations that pierced the veil between the mortal and the divine, bestowing upon Aquinas insights so profound, they shaped the very essence of his theological oeuvre. Such divine encounters fortified his convictions and emboldened his pen, allowing him to craft arguments of unparalleled cogency and depth. Even as skeptics might scoff and dissenters dispute, none can deny the transformative impact these divine revelations had upon Aquinas's work, embedding within it a sacredness that mere human reasoning alone could never achieve. In laying bare the mystical experiences of Aquinas, we venture into the heart of his sanctity, witnessing the divine hand that guided his intellect and proving, beyond a shadow of a doubt, that knowledge, in its truest form, serveth faithfully at the feet of faith.

The Impact on His Work When divine revelations touched the soul of Thomas Aquinas, their profound impact did verily transcend the mortal realms of understanding and reason, guiding his prolific hand in the crafting of works that sought to bridge the ethereal gap betwixt Heaven and Earth. These celestial encounters, whispered to him in moments of deep spiritual communion, did serve as both a muse and a divine compass, directing his scholarly pursuits with a heavenly light.

Though Aquinas was a man of immense intellectual prowess, these mystical experiences did cast a luminous glow upon his work, imbuing it with an essence that mere human wisdom alone could not achieve. The profundity of these revelations did not simply augment his academic endeavors but transformed them, infusing his rigorous analyses and dialectical discourses with an otherworldly insight.

In the hallowed halls of academia and the sacred spaces of the church, his writings, once perceived as mere scholastic exercises, came to be revered as conduits of divine wisdom. Through his pen, complex theological concepts were demystified, and the presence of the Almighty was made palpable to those who sought understanding. His oeuvre became a beacon, guiding souls towards the divine light, and fostering a deeper, more intimate relationship with the Creator.

Aquinas, in his quest for divine knowledge, did not shy away from the formidable challenges that lay before him. He wrestled with the grand mysteries of existence, employing reason and faith as his steadfast companions. Yet, it was through his mystical experiences that he gleaned the most profound insights, insights that would illuminate the darkest corners of doubt and ignorance.

His magnum opus, the Summa Theologica, serves as a testament to the indelible impact of these divine encounters. Within its pages lies a harmonious symphony of faith and reason, a magisterial effort to articulate the truths of the Christian faith with unparalleled clarity and depth. Each question posed, each answer provided, reflects the divine guidance that steered Aquinas's scholarly journey, making the Summa not only a work of theological brilliance but a vessel of divine revelation.

The mystical experiences that graced Aquinas also bestowed upon him a profound humility, a recognition of the vast expanse of divine mystery that lay beyond the reach of human comprehension. This humility permeated his work, reminding all who would follow in his intellectual footsteps that, despite the vastness of our knowledge, we stand but on the shoreline of the infinite ocean of God's wisdom.

Notwithstanding, these celestial encounters did also present Aquinas with a dilemma of unparalleled gravity. How does one continue the work of reason and writing when faced with the ineffable majesty of God's direct revelation? This question did plague his later years, leading him to famously declare his written works as "straw" compared to the glory of God's revelation.

His decision to cease writing, following a particularly profound mystical experience, marks a pivotal moment in his life and work. It signifies the ultimate surrender of the intellect to the divine will, an acknowledgment that the quest for knowledge, however noble, pales in comparison to the direct experience of God's presence.

Yet, even in his silence, Aquinas's work continued to speak volumes. The legacy of his writing, shaped and sanctified by his mystical experiences, has endured through the centuries, offering light and guidance to those who seek to navigate the treacherous waters of doubt and disbelief.

The impact of Aquinas's work, therefore, cannot be overstated. His theological and philosophical contributions do not merely represent the pinnacle of scholastic achievement; they are a clarion call to all who seek understanding, inviting them to embark on their own journey towards divine wisdom.

In a world often ensnared by the illusion of materialism and the echoes of skepticism, Aquinas's writings stand as a testament to the enduring power of faith. They remind us that at the heart of true knowledge lies not the accumulation of facts and arguments, but a living, breathing relationship with the divine.

Thus, the mystical experiences of Thomas Aquinas did not merely shape his work; they transformed it, elevating it from the realm of scholarly pursuit to an act of divine worship. In his efforts to articulate the mysteries of faith, he became a bridge between Heaven and Earth, guiding countless souls towards the light of understanding and belief.

The significance of Aquinas's work, enriched and enlivened by his encounters with the divine, extends far beyond the confines of history. It stands as a beacon of hope and a source of wisdom for all who seek to reconcile the demands of reason with the call of faith.

In this age of uncertainty and searching, the life and works of Thomas Aquinas, guided by divine revelation, offer a compelling testament to the power of faith. They challenge us to open our hearts to the mystical, to dare to believe that beyond the veil of the visible lies an infinite realm of divine truth waiting to be discovered.

Let us, then, take up the mantle of inquiry and faith that Aquinas has bequeathed to us, embarking on our own quest for divine wisdom. For in the teachings of this great saint, we find not only a path to knowledge but a gateway to the heart of God Himself.

The Decision to Cease Writing

In the twilit years of his life, as recounted in the annals of our spiritual heritage, Thomas Aquinas encountered the divine in such a profound manner that the e'er resplendent tapestry of his theological musings paled in comparison. 'Twas in the midst of composing his magnum opus, the Summa Theologica, that the ethereal veil was lifted, and Aquinas found himself at the threshold of the ineffable. These celestial revelations, bestowed upon him with such clarity and intensity, led him to utter in solemnity, "All that I have written seems like straw." This stark pronouncement signified not a repudiation of his life's work but rather an acknowledgment of the immeasurable grandeur of the Almighty sensed through his mystical experiences. Thereafter, he laid down his quill, ceasing the pursuit of further writings. His decision, enveloped in the gravitas of his spiritual awakening, serves as a reverent testimonium to the belief that beyond the realm of human understanding and expression lies the true essence of the divine, accessible not through the intellect alone but through the soul's profound communion with God.

"All That I Have Written Seems Like Straw" Verily, the words of Thomas, upon the twilight of his days, have stirred the cores of many a scholar, theologian, and seeker of truth. Tis a tale most profound, a revelation that beckons unto the depths of humility and insight alike. For what prompted such a declaration from one deemed a colossus in the realm of intellect?

In sooth, the journey of Thomas Aquinas, marked by the quest for understanding, for bridging the chasm betwixt faith and reason, didst take a turn most unexpected. Following a divine revelation, experienced during the celebration of Mass, the very fabric of his perception was irrevocably altered. What visions, what whisperings of the divine might have transpired? Mortal ken mayhap cannot grasp; yet, the impact was such that he professed his opus, the very culmination of his life's toil, to be as naught but straw.

Consider, if thou wilt, the gravity of such a declaration. Here stood a man, a pillar of thought and devoutness, whose works were as a beacon unto those seeking clarity in matters of faith and scholarship. The Summa Theologica, a monumental endeavor, sought to encompass the entirety of theological knowledge of the age. Yet, in a moment of epiphanic clarity, tempered perhaps by the divine touch, Thomas beheld his work as lacking.

What, then, dost this signify for those of us enmeshed in the pursuit of knowledge? Thomas's revelation, far from discrediting his scholarly achievements, illumines the path of humility. It echoes the eternal truth that, in the presence of the Divine, the pinnacle of human wisdom but grazes the surface. The quest for understanding, though noble and just, finds its culmination not in the annals of human intellect but in the embrace of faith.

For scholars, theologians, and students alike, there lies a profound lesson in the heart of Thomas's revelation. It serves as a reminder that, no matter the heights of intellect we may scale, our comprehension of the divine mystery is ever partial, ever limited. The true essence of wisdom, then, lieth not in the amassing of knowledge but in the recognition of its limits, in the bowing of the head and the bending of the knee before the ineffable majesty of God.

This moment of profound humility and insight didst not diminish Thomas's legacy; rather, it ennobles it. By acknowledging the limitations of his work in the light of divine revelation, Thomas Aquinas exemplifies the true end of all scholarly endeavor: to draw us closer to the divine, to deepen our faith through the use of reason, yet always aware of its confines.

Let us, therefore, grapple with the implications of Thomas's epiphany. It is a clarion call to approach our studies, our teachings, our very lives with humility. In every question explored, in every answer sought, there lies an invitation to look beyond the confines of human understanding, to the divine Source of all wisdom.

In the annals of history, Thomas's decision to cease his writings following this revelation may appear as a retreat from scholarship. Yet, in truth, it is a profound act of faith, a testament to his unshakeable belief in the supremacy of divine knowledge over human understanding. It challenges us, in our ceaseless quests for knowledge, to recognize the moment when silence becomes the most eloquent testimony to the truth.

The legacy of Thomas Aquinas, thus, extends far beyond the texts and treatises that bear his name. It lies in the enduring relevance of his journey, a journey from knowledge to wisdom, from scholarship to faith. As we navigate the complexities of the modern world, his life and works stand as beacons, guiding us towards a deeper, more nuanced understanding of the relationship between faith and reason.

In this world teeming with knowledge, where the boundaries of what is knowable are ever expanding, Thomas's revelation invites us to pause, to reflect on the ultimate purpose of our quest for understanding. It beckons us to consider that, at the very heart of all scholarly endeavor, there must lie a deeper yearning: the yearning for truth, for meaning, for a glimpse of the divine.

Thus, as we tread the path of knowledge, let us do so with the humility and insight that Thomas Aquinas exemplified. Let us strive, in all our endeavors, to discern not only the workings of the world but also the whispers of the divine. And, in our moments of revelation, may we too have the courage to acknowledge the limits of our understanding, to see our work as straw in comparison to the transcendence and majesty of God's eternal wisdom.

In the end, the words of Thomas Aquinas serve not as a repudiation of his life's work but as a culmination, a turning point that beckons us towards a deeper engagement with the mysteries of faith. They remind us that the ultimate goal of our scholarly and spiritual quests is not found in the accumulation of knowledge but in the humble acknowledgement of its limits before the boundless expanse of the divine.

Mayhap, then, as we delve into the rich legacy of Thomas Aquinas, we can uncover not only the brilliance of his mind but also the depth of his faith. In his works, as vast and varied as they are, we find a journey—a journey that leads us, ultimately, to the heart of wisdom. And in the acknowledgment that all he had written seemed like straw, we find a profound invitation to seek beyond the written word, to the Word made flesh, to Jesus, in whom all our quests find their end and their fulfillment.

Let this narrative not only stand as a testament to Thomas Aquinas's intellectual and spiritual journey but also serve as a lodestar for our own paths. In his humility, in his ceaseless pursuit of truth, may we find the courage to confront our limitations, to embrace the mysteries of faith, and to seek, always, the face of God.

The Legacy of Thomas Aquinas

As we transition from the mystical realm of Aquinas's celestial experiences into the echoing halls of his enduring legacy, it is clear that the profound spirit of Thomas Aquinas pervades the very fabric of modern thought and sanctity. Amidst the tempest of temporal progression, his philosophical edifice stands as a beacon of divine intellect, casting luminous rays upon both theology and philosophy. In the annals of history, his virtuous life hath been canonized, not merely within the venerated chapters of ecclesiastical doctrine but in the heart of Christendom itself, where miracles attributed to his intercession affirm his sainthood. Yet, 'tis not solely in the ethereal or miraculous that his influence doth manifest, but also in the vigorous debates of morality, ethics, and the essence of existence that grace our contemporary agora. His teachings, once the clarion call against heresies, now serve as a bridge betwixt faith and reason, illuminating paths for scholars, theologians, and laypersons alike in their quest for celestial truth. Thus, in the contemplation of Aquinas's legacy, one discovers not merely a relic of a bygone era but a living testament to the unity of human inquiry and divine revelation, a testimony that speaks with undiminished relevance to this day.

Aquinas in the Modern World

In this present age, where the clamor of worldly affairs oft drowns the gentle whispers of faith, the legacy of Thomas Aquinas stands as a beacon of divine reason amidst the tumult. His teachings, deeply rooted in the harmonious interplay of faith and reason, continue to illuminate the path for those who, in their search for truth, find themselves at the crossroads of doubt and belief. Aquinas' profound insights into the nature of God, the universe, and the human soul resonate with a startling relevance, offering a compass for navigating the complexities of modern life. His Summa Theologica, a monumental work that once bridged the medieval and the divine, now speaks to the hearts of the contemporary faithful, guiding them through the fog of skepticism and relativism. For scholars and theologians, the study of Aquinas' works is not a mere academic pursuit, but a journey towards understanding the intricate tapestry of existence through the eyes of one who beheld the face of God. As the world evolves, so too does the interpretation of his writings, each generation discovering fresh insights and wisdom within. Thus, in the ceaseless flux of human thought and experience, the legacy of Thomas Aquinas endures, a timeless testament to the enduring power of faith informed by reason.

Influence on Theology and Philosophy As we venture further into the legacy of Thomas Aquinas, we encounter a realm wherein his mark is indelibly imprinted upon the discourse of theology and philosophy. His intellect, akin to a beacon of divine radiance, hath illuminated the path for countless souls who seek to comprehend the nature of God and His creation. This section aims to explore the profound impact of Aquinas's work on the realms of theology and philosophy, an influence that reacheth beyond the confines of his own era and extendeth unto the present day.

In the annals of history, few have managed to weave together the threads of faith and reason as masterfully as Aquinas. It was his steadfast belief that there existeth no true discord between the divine revelations granted by faith and the truths discovered through human reason. This proposition, revolutionary in its time, hath laid the foundations for a harmonious relationship between theology and philosophy. In focusing on this relationship, one discerns the silhouette of Aquinas's influence, guiding discourse in both fields with an assurance born of divine inspiration.

One cannot discuss Aquinas's impact on theology without delving into his magnum opus, the *Summa Theologica*. Within its pages, Aquinas embarked upon a meticulous exploration of the Christian faith, employing a philosophical framework to articulate and defend its doctrines. His method, known as Scholasticism, became a cornerstone for theological debate and education. Through his works, Aquinas hath demonstrated that rigorous intellectual inquiry and devout faith not only can coexist but indeed flourish together, enlightening one another.

Moreover, Aquinas's philosophical explorations, particularly concerning metaphysics and ethics, have left an indelible mark upon Western thought. His conception of being, essence, and existence has shaped the philosophical discourse, offering a robust framework for understanding the underpinnings of reality. By asserting that being itself participates in the divine essence, Aquinas provided philosophers with a bridge from the temporal to the eternal, a pathway leading from the contingent towards the Absolute.

The influence of Aquinas also permeates the realm of moral philosophy, where his virtue ethics continue to offer guidance. In positing that virtuous living aligns with human nature's fulfillment, Aquinas provided a moral compass pointing toward the good life. This emphasis on virtue as the pathway to human flourishing hath found resonance in contemporary ethics, informing debates on the nature of happiness, moral character, and the good society.

Furthermore, Aquinas's reconciliation of Aristotelian philosophy with Christian theology opened new avenues for intellectual engagement. By demonstrating the compatibility of faith with the philosophical heritage of the Greeks, Aquinas bridged worlds, enriching Christian thought with the insights of Aristotle and his compatriots. This synthesis hath inspired scholars and theologians to seek wisdom in the confluence of diverse intellectual traditions, fostering a spirit of openness and dialogue.

In addition, Aquinas's contributions to natural theology, particularly his Five Ways of demonstrating God's existence, have provided a rational foundation for faith. These arguments, leveraging observations from the natural world to infer the existence of a divine Creator, have been instrumental in apologetics, aiming to show that belief in God is supported by reason as well as revelation.

His discourse on the nature of angels, though seemingly esoteric, hath offered profound insights into the understanding of immaterial beings and their role within the cosmic order. Through such discussions, Aquinas enriched the theological imagination, inviting contemplation of the mysteries that dwell beyond the veil of the material world.

The egalitarian notion that truth can be discovered by anyone, regardless of their state in life, was ardently championed by Aquinas. This democratization of knowledge, advocating for the accessibility of truth to all who seek it with a sincere heart, hath implications far beyond theology and philosophy. It asserteth a profound respect for the intellectual potential of every individual, challenging elitist notions of knowledge and learning.

Aquinas's influence extendeth also to the discourse on law and governance. In his treatises, he explored the principles of just law and the moral obligations of rulers, offering insights that remain relevant in discussions of political ethics and the rule of law. His vision of a society governed by laws that reflect the natural law and divine order continues to inspire those who seek justice in human affairs.

In the context of education, the Thomistic method of question and answer, of dialogue and dialectic, hath profoundly shaped pedagogical approaches. By fostering an environment wherein questions are encouraged and knowledge is pursued through reasoned argument, Aquinas contributed to the development of a more critical and reflective mode of education.

The mystical dimensions of Aquinas's thought, though perhaps lesser-known, offer a window into the contemplative aspect of his theology. His writings on mysticism and the beatific vision highlight the ultimate aim of human life as union with the divine. These works invite the faithful to explore the depths of spiritual life, emphasizing the transformative power of divine love.

In the ecclesial domain, Aquinas's theology hath served as a bedrock for the Roman Catholic Church's doctrinal teachings. The Councils of Trent and Vatican II, among others, have drawn upon his work to articulate and defend the faith against challenges from within and without. His influence thus percolates through the Church's magisterial documents, catechism, and liturgical practices.

Lastly, Aquinas's legacy acts as a beacon for those engaged in interfaith dialogue. His respect for truth, wherever it may be found, and his engagement with the works of Muslim and Jewish scholars, exemplify a spirit of openness and respect for the other. In an era marked by religious pluralism, Aquinas's example encourages fruitful dialogue and mutual learning among diverse faith traditions.

In sum, the influence of Thomas Aquinas on theology and philosophy is as a river that exceeds its banks, nourishing diverse fields of inquiry and practice. His life's work, a testament to the harmony between faith and reason, continues to enlighten minds and kindle hearts, guiding them toward that ultimate truth which alone satisfies the human soul's longing.

The Sainthood

In the annals of Christendom, few luminaries shine as brightly as Thomas Aquinas, whose earthly sojourn, replete with toils for the Kingdom of Light, did not conclude at his departure from this mortal coil but found its zenith in the hallowed recognition of sainthood. After his departure, myriad faithful bore witness to miracles wrought through his intercession, a testament not merely to the sanctity of his life but to the enduring power of his faith and works. The Church, in her wisdom, recognizing the profound impact of his theological contributions and the purity of his devotion, embarked upon the rigorous process of canonization. In 1323, less than half a century post his passing, Aquinas was canonized by Pope John XXII, a swift acknowledgment by the ecclesiastical standards of the day, which bespoke the immensity of his spiritual and intellectual legacy. His feast day, initially observed on the day of his rest, was later moved to January 28, the day of his relics' translation, further immortalizing his contribution to the Catholic faith. This apotheosis, a crowning jewel atop his manifold achievements, serves not merely as a veneration of the man but as a beacon of divine brilliance, guiding the faithful toward the harmonious coexistence of faith and reason, and ultimately, toward a fuller understanding of the Divine.

Miracles and Canonization In the annals of yon venerated Church, wherein tales of grace and divine intercession weave like threads of gold through the fabric of history, the account of Saint Thomas Aquinas stands as a bastion of faith's triumph over worldliness. Verily, the process of canonization, that hallowed rite which doth elevate men to the ranks of saints, oft hinges upon the manifestation of miracles, signs of the Almighty's favor and the sanctity of the individual. So it was with Aquinas, whose life, whilst rich in intellectual conquests, was also marked by occurrences that transcend mere mortal understanding.

Forsooth, the Church requireth miracles for canonization, a testament to the candidate's union with the divine, thus proving their worthiness of universal veneration. The miracles attributed to Thomas, posthumously recorded and rigorously examined, speak volumes of his enduring influence in the realm unseen as much as in the scholastic endeavors he undertook whilst amongst the living.

Prior to his canonization, numerous accounts of miraculous interventions were meticulously scrutinized, for the Church, in its wisdom, demands evidence most clear and unassailable. Among these, healings unexplainable by the art of medicine of the time, interventions in moments of dire need, and appearances in visions granting solace and guidance to the faithful were most prominent. These occurrences, documented by those who bore witness, provided the bedrock upon which his sainthood was later declared.

It is told that on a night most dark, when a tempest threatened to swallow a vessel whole, sailors, despairing, called upon Aquinas's intercession. Lo, the storm abated, replaced by a calm as sudden as it was inexplicable, thus saving those aboard from certain doom. Such tales of deliverance through his intercession abound, each serving as a beacon of hope for those who, as shadows encroach upon their hearts, seek light.

In matters of the flesh, too, his miracles were manifest. The sick, the lame, and the blind, having sought his aid through fervent prayer, oft found their maladies cured, their burdens lifted by an unseen hand. Each healing, each return from the brink of despair, was meticulously recorded, subjected to the scrutiny of those appointed by the Church to judge the veracity of such claims.

Yet, the path to canonization is fraught with rigor, for the Church, in its role as shepherd to the faithful, doth not hastily confer sainthood. The process did unfold over years, nay, decades, testament to the solemnity with which this sacred duty is undertaken. Investigations, deliberations, and the seeking of Divine confirmation through prayer preceded the final declaration, ensuring that no doubt could linger concerning Aquinas's sanctity and the validity of the miracles ascribed to him.

Upon the consummation of this rigorous examination, it came to pass that Thomas Aquinas was canonized, enshrined amongst those exalted few whose lives and works continue to inspire, guide, and intercede for humanity. This esteemed recognition not only solidified his place within the annals of the Church but also served as an indelible testament to the inextricable link between faith and reason, between the earthly scholarship and divine wisdom.

The canonization of Aquinas, occurring in the year of our Lord 1323, less than fifty years after his departure from this mortal coil, was met with jubilation across Christendom. It was a vindication, a celestial endorsement of his life's work, a beacon to all who pursue truth in the shadow of faith. Thus, the veneration of Aquinas was not merely for the intellect that sought to comprehend the incomprehensible but also for the spirit that touched the heart of the Divine.

In the grand tapestry of the Church's history, the miracles and canonization of Saint Thomas Aquinas serve as a reminder that sanctity and scholarship can coalesce, that one's endeavors in the realm of thought are not divorced from the spiritual, but indeed may lead one closer to the Divine. His sainthood stands as a symbol, a bridge between the heavenly and the earthly, illustrating that the pursuit of knowledge, when undertaken with a heart open to God's grace, can itself be an act of devotion.

The miracles attributed to Saint Thomas Aquinas, thus, are not merely relics of a bygone era, signs and wonders to be marveled at from afar. Nay, they are living testaments to the vitality of faith, enduring proofs that the divine hand doth still move within our world, guiding, healing, and affirming the bond between the Creator and His creation.

As scholars and laypeople alike delve into the life and works of Aquinas, they are beckoned to reflect upon the miracles that punctuated his path to sainthood. In these divine interventions, there is a message of hope, a confirmation that the heavens are not deaf to our pleas, that saints, like Aquinas, continue to intercede on behalf of humanity, channeling the boundless mercy of God.

The narrative of Saint Thomas Aquinas, embellished by the miraculous and crowned by canonization, thus serves not merely as historical account or theological discourse. It is a beacon, illuminating the path toward a fuller understanding of the divine mystery, inviting all to recognize in Aquinas not only the scholar or saint but the profound intercessor who bridges our world and the next.

In conclusion, the miracles and canonization of Saint Thomas Aquinas stand as a testament to the enduring power of faith, an exemplar of how divine grace can work through human intellect and piety. As believers and seekers of knowledge draw inspiration from his life, may they also find solace in the miracles that affirm his sanctity, seeing in them the hand of God at work in our world, leading us ever onward toward enlightenment and salvation.

Chapter 11: Revisiting Aquinas in Contemporary Debates

As we hath trod the path through the dense forests of history, bearing witness to the illustrious tale and enduring legacy of Saint Thomas Aquinas, we find ourselves at the crossroads of yore and today in Chapter 11. It is here, amidst the clamor and din of modern discourse, that the timeless wisdom of Aquinas doth shine as a beacon of enlightenment. With deft and profound insight, Aquinas bridged the seemingly vast chasm 'twixt faith and reason, proffering arguments that yet hold sway in the raging debates of science and moral philosophy. His opus, rooted in the belief that veritas - truth, is a divine illumination accessible to the human intellect, challenges us to reconsider the underpinnings of ethical conduct and the natural world. In an age where the fabric of moral society is oft in disarray, tangled in the web of technological advancement and relativism, Aquinas's discourse on virtues and his quintessential Five Ways to prove the existence of God serve not merely as an intellectual exercise, but as a guiding compass. As we navigate through the tempests of today's ethical dilemmas and the quest for harmony between scientific discovery and spiritual belief, Aquinas stands as a towering figure whose thoughts kindle a light of wisdom, guiding the soul towards a haven where faith dances in concert with reason, and truth, unshackled from the constraints of temporal disputes, reaches towards the divine.

Aquinas and Science

In the bygone era, where shadows of ignorance stretched across the minds of men, there emerged a beacon of light, Thomas Aquinas, whose genius traversed the realms of theology and science, intertwining them in a harmonious embrace. This section unfolds the story of how Aquinas, with the acumen of a sage and the devotion of a saint, sought to bridge the chasm between faith and reason. Verily, in his esteemed work, Aquinas demonstrated that the natural world, governed by laws and principles, was not at odds with the divine but a testament to its Creator's grandeur. He posited that truth, whether revealed through scripture or discerned from the natural order, flowed from the same divine fountain, compelling those of devout faith and rigorous inquiry to marvel at the coherence between the cosmos and the Creator. Aquinas's approach heralded a departure from the darkened perceptions of his age, suggesting that the study of the natural world could lead the inquisitive soul closer to God, thus sanctifying the pursuit of knowledge as an act of devotion. His legacy, a tapestry of scholastic insight, remains a cornerstone for those who seek to understand the divine through the lens of reason and the natural sciences, proving that faith and empirical inquiry are not foes but allies in the quest for truth.

Bridging the Gap Between Faith and Reason Verily, as we traverse the boundless realms of knowledge and belief, a venture most sublime awaits those who seek to unravel the mysteries betwixt faith and reason. In the age of Aquinas, a luminary did emerge, whose intellect and spirit sought to unite the seemingly disparate worlds of divine revelation and human understanding.

It hath been said that reason and faith dwell in constant strife, locked in an eternal battle for the souls of men. Yet, Aquinas perceived not a battlefield, but a garden, wherein reason and faith might flourish together, each nourishing the other to yield the fruits of wisdom.

In his quest for truth, Aquinas embarked upon a journey most profound, navigating the chasm that many believed impassable. He argued that reason, in its purest form, is a gift from the Divine, a beacon that guides us toward the eternal light of understanding.

The scholastic sage posited that all truth, whether revealed through scripture or discovered via rational inquiry, emanates from the same source—God Almighty. Hence, contradictions between faith and reason are but illusions, mirages that fade under the scrutiny of diligent study and contemplative prayer.

The Five Ways, Aquinas' masterful exposition on the existence of God, exemplifies this harmonious convergence of faith and reason. With the precision of a philosopher and the conviction of a devout believer, he unveils the logical necessity of a Prime Mover, an Uncaused Cause, a Being of perfect goodness, from which all creation flows.

Yet, the sage of Aquin cautions us that reason alone cannot fathom the entirety of divine mystery. For there exist truths beyond the grasp of human intellect, sacred mysteries that are known solely through the grace of faith. Thus, reason acts as the handmaid to faith, escorting the soul to the threshold of divine revelation.

In the discourse of Aquinas, one finds a profound affirmation of the human capacity to know God through the natural light of reason, a notion that challenged the prevailing scepticism of his time. He argued that our senses, though fallible, are windows to the truth, and our reason, though finite, has the power to apprehend the immutable laws that govern creation.

Through the annals of history, this endeavor to reconcile faith with reason has ignited the minds of scholars and theologians alike, inspiring a pursuit of knowledge that is at once rigorous and devout. Aquinas taught that in the quest for truth, one must employ both the lantern of reason and the compass of faith, for together they illuminate the path to enlightenment.

In contemporary times, the discourse Aquinas initiated continues to bear relevance, as science and religion often find themselves at odds. Yet, through the Thomistic lens, we discern that faith and reason are not adversaries but allies in the exploration of reality.

Aquinas' legacy serves as a beacon to those who navigate the tumultuous seas of doubt and belief, offering a model of intellectual humility and openness. He reminds us that the pursuit of truth is a journey that encompasses both the empirical and the transcendental, the observable and the revealed.

As we contemplate the vastness of the cosmos and the intricacies of the natural world, the voice of Aquinas whispers to us across the ages, urging us to seek the divine harmony that resides in the unity of faith and reason. He calls upon us to embrace the complexity of this quest, for in its resolution lies the essence of wisdom.

The admonitions and insights of Aquinas challenge us to rise above the discord and division that often characterise the discourse between science and religion. He beckons us to a higher plane of understanding, wherein we may acknowledge the limitations of our knowledge while rejoicing in the boundless beauty of creation that faith and reason together reveal.

In this era of skepticism and relativism, the teachings of Aquinas shine forth as a testament to the enduring power of faith informed by reason. His vision of a synthesis between the natural and the divine offers hope to those who yearn for a more profound comprehension of their existence and purpose.

Therefore, let us tread the path blazed by Aquinas, wherein the mind and the spirit journey together in search of the ultimate truth. For in the embrace of faith and reason, we find not only the answers to our most pressing questions but also the peace that surpasses all understanding.

Thus concludes our exploration of the sacred interplay between faith and reason, a theme that has captivated the hearts and minds of humanity through the ages. May the wisdom of Aquinas guide us as we continue our quest for knowledge and meaning in a world that yearns for the light of truth.

Moral Philosophy and Ethics

In the tapestry of contemporary discourses, the threads of Aquinas's moral philosophy and ethics emerge as guidestars, illuminating pathways through the moral quandaries of our era. For in the wisdom of Aquinas, we find not merely an ancient doctrine, but a living dialogue with the present, a compass by which to navigate the complex moral landscapes we tread. At the heart of his teachings lies the conviction that moral actions spring from virtuous habits, nurtured by a steadfast adherence to reason and divine law. Aquinas posits that the virtues - both moral, such as prudence and justice, and intellectual, like wisdom and understanding - form the bedrock of ethical living. In an age beset by relativism and the fragmentation of moral consensus, Aquinas's emphasis on natural law and the universality of moral truths offers a beacon of certainty. By engaging deeply with his ethics, scholars, theologians, and laypersons alike are beckoned to explore how virtue ethics can be applied within the modern context, providing a bulwark against the moral drift that plagues contemporary society. Thus, in the burgeoning discourse on moral philosophy and ethics, Aquinas's legacy endures, a testament to the enduring relevance of Thomistic thought in guiding the moral compass of today's world.

Guidance in Today's World In the ever-evolving tapestry of human existence, where modernity and tradition oft clash in a tumultuous dance, the teachings and principles of Thomas Aquinas stand as a beacon of light, guiding the faithful and ponderous through the murky waters of contemporary moral conundrums. As we navigate the complexities of our age, the wisdom of Aquinas, though ancient, speaks with a surprising relevance to the issues that touch the very core of our lives.

In matters of ethics and morality, the world finds itself at a crossroads, confronted with a barrage of dilemmas that demand not only intellectual rigor but a heart anchored in steadfast virtue. Aquinas, in his profound synthesis of faith and reason, offers us a compass by which to orient our moral compass amidst the storms of relativism and nihilism that threaten to unsettle the very foundations of our moral landscape.

The principle of the natural law, as expounded by Aquinas, asserts that certain rights and wrongs are inscribed in the very nature of humanity, accessible to reason and reflective of a higher divine law. This notion, far from being a relic of a bygone era, provides a robust framework for engaging with contemporary ethical issues, from the sanctity of life to the complexities of social justice and human rights.

Consider the debates that rage around the issues of life and death—abortion, euthanasia, capital punishment. Aquinas teaches us that life is a sacred gift from God, imbued with inherent dignity and value. His teachings challenge us to view these issues not through the lens of personal autonomy or societal benefit alone but within the context of a moral order that transcends our transient desires and opinions.

In the sphere of social justice, Aquinas's emphasis on the common good and the necessity of charity in the distribution of wealth speaks poignantly to the challenges of poverty, inequality, and exploitation that confront our globalized world. His understanding of justice as giving each their due, grounded in a profound respect for the human person, offers a corrective to both unfettered capitalism and reductive socialism.

In the realm of politics, Aquinas's vision of governance, grounded in the pursuit of the common good and informed by moral virtue, offers a counterpoint to the cynicism and pragmatism that often characterizes contemporary political life. His belief in the importance of laws that are just, promoting the moral and spiritual welfare of the community, challenges us to envision a politics that is not merely about power or efficiency but about fostering a society reflective of our highest ideals.

The question of human sexuality and relationships, fraught with controversy and division in today's world, is another area where Aquinas's teachings provide valuable insight. His understanding of human sexuality within the context of marriage and procreation, as well as his recognition of the unitive dimension of the sexual act, invites a deeper reflection on the meaning and purpose of our sexual nature in a culture often obsessed with personal gratification and freedom from constraint.

On environmental ethics, the respect for creation that underpins Thomistic thought calls us to a stewardship that recognizes the intrinsic value of the natural world and our responsibility to preserve it for future generations. In an age of ecological crisis, Aquinas's integrative vision of the cosmos as a sacramental reality, reflecting the beauty and goodness of its Creator, provides a theological foundation for ecological action that is deeply needed.

In the pursuit of knowledge and truth, Aquinas's dedication to the life of the intellect and his confidence in the ability of human reason to apprehend reality challenge the skepticism and subjectivism that often characterize postmodern thought. His belief in the complementarity of faith and reason offers a path for reconciling science and religion, philosophy, and theology in the search for a coherent and comprehensive understanding of the world and our place within it.

Aquinas's commitment to dialogue and engagement with thinkers outside the Christian tradition, notably his incorporation of Aristotle and other Greek philosophers into his theological framework, serves as a model for interfaith dialogue and the pursuit of universal truths across cultural and religious divides. In a world marked by religious conflict and intolerance, the Thomistic approach to truth, grounded in respect and openness to the other, is more pertinent than ever.

In matters of personal development and virtue, the Thomistic emphasis on the cultivation of the virtues—prudence, justice, fortitude, and temperance, among others—as the path to human flourishing provides a timeless guide for character formation in a culture that often celebrates vice as virtue. Aquinas reminds us that true happiness is found not in the accumulation of material wealth or the pursuit of pleasure but in living a life oriented toward the good, the true, and the beautiful.

Finally, in the quest for meaning and purpose that animates every human heart, Aquinas's synthesis of Christian theology with the philosophical pursuit of truth invites us to a deeper exploration of the questions that define our existence: Who are we? Why are we here? What is our ultimate destiny? His assurance that our deepest longings find their fulfillment in the knowledge and love of God offers a beacon of hope in an age of uncertainty and despair.

In sum, the wisdom of Thomas Aquinas, steeped in the depths of the Christian intellectual tradition, provides not only a rich resource for engaging with the ethical challenges of our time but also a luminous path toward a life of virtue, wisdom, and joy. In a world hungering for meaning, direction, and truth, the teachings of Aquinas stand as a testament to the enduring power of faith illuminated by reason, guiding us toward the ultimate source of all light, Jesus Christ, the incarnate Word of God.

Thus, as we sojourn through the shifting sands of time, the enduring legacy of Thomas Aquinas offers not merely an academic or historical curiosity but a living wellspring of wisdom and grace, beckoning us to drink deeply and be refreshed in our quest for the way, the truth, and the life.

Chapter 12: Thomism and Interfaith Dialogue

In the grand tapestry of discourse that is woven through the ages, a singular thread of Thomistic thought finds its way into the heart of interfaith dialogue, a testament to the enduring reverence for Saint Thomas Aquinas and his unmatched intellect. This chapter doth unravel the intricacies of how Thomism art a catalyst for bridging the vast divides betwixt diverse faiths, championing a mutual quest for understanding and respect. Aquinas, in his boundless wisdom, argued not for the supremacy of one creed over another but for the pursuit of universal truths and shared values, anchoring such endeavors in a foundation of philosophical rigor and theological depth. 'Tis a tale of how religious tolerance and the engagement with 'the other' are not merely acts of modern diplomatic necessity but are deeply rooted in the Thomistic tradition. Aquinas, with his unparalleled ability to engage with the works of thinkers both near and distant to his own doctrinal backgrounds, exemplifies how dialogue is not a compromise of faith but an extension of it. In a world rife with discord, the principles of Thomism shine as a beacon of hope, advocating for an intellectual exchange that transcends the mere tolerance of differences, aiming instead for a harmonious concord among all peoples, regardless of creed. Thus, Thomism doth proffer a noble pathway to peace, through earnest and respectful dialogue, grounded in the belief that, beneath the myriad ways in which humanity seeks the divine, lies a common yearning for truth and goodness.

Lessons in Religious Tolerance

In the annals of history, where scholars and theologians oft entwine in discourse, a chapter standeth out, whispering lessons of forbearance and peace—the teachings of Aquinas on the dignity of engaging with the 'Other.' In times of great divide, where beliefs clash and discord reigns, his wisdom, like a beacon, lights our path towards understanding. For Thomas didst not shun those of differing faiths but sought to comprehend their essence, to find amidst the cacophony of beliefs, a melody of shared humanity. This quest for knowledge and understanding, borne not of mere curiosity but of a deep-seated respect for all God's creations, doth teach us that in dialogue, not diatribe, we find our common ground. So let us tread softly in his philosophic steps, embracing those who walk paths divergent from our own, for in each heart burns the same quest for truth. This act of reaching out, of listening and learning, forms the cornerstone of religious tolerance, a testament to the belief that wisdom's garden thriveth best when nourished by the many, not the few.

Engaging with the Other As we tread further into the essence of Thomistic theology, it becomes imperative to explore the Unity of Truth in its relation to religious tolerance, a virtue Saint Thomas Aquinas esteemed highly in his quest for divine understanding. Fain would he engage in discourse with those of differing beliefs, not as adversaries but as fellow seekers of truth. This chapter endeavours to illuminate how Aquinas, through devout faith and unparalleled intellect, sought to engage with proponents of divergent theological and philosophical perspectives.

In the time of Aquinas, Christendom was not a stranger to conflict within its borders and with those beyond. Yet, in such times as these, Aquinas emerged as a beacon of hope, demonstrating through his words and deeds that engagement with the other was not only possible but necessary for the advancement of truth. The mendicant friar, though steadfast in his own faith, was known for his willingness to traverse the intellectual landscapes of Islam, Judaism, and even the then-emerging humanist thought, seeking always to understand before seeking to be understood.

The scholarly exchanges at the University of Paris bore witness to the inclusivity of Aquinas's approach. It was here that the doctrine of "faith seeking understanding" took flight, as Aquinas posited that all truth, no matter its source, ultimately emanates from the Divine. Thus, he argued, engaging with ideas foreign to Christian doctrine could not endanger the faith, but only deepen and enrich it.

A pivotal aspect of Aquinas's engagement with the other was his unrivalled mastery of the works of Aristotle. Though the Philosopher, as he was known, predated Christendom, Aquinas revered Aristotle's works as a monumental edifice of human reason. This appropriation and interpretation of Aristotle served as a bridge between Christian and classical thought, illustrating that truth, irrespective of its origin, is universal.

The manner of Aquinas's engagement was marked by respect and earnestness. He understood that to convert one must first converse, to illuminate one must first listen. In his disputations, Aquinas never shied away from presenting the strength of an opposing argument, trusting that the light of truth, if it were truly so, would shine all the brighter in juxtaposition.

Through such dialogues, Aquinas exemplified that faith and reason are not adversaries but allies in the quest for understanding. This principle found its embodiment in his most lauded work, the Summa Theologica, where he employed reason to elucidate and defend the tenets of faith. This magnum opus stands as a testament to the unity of truth and the possibility of engaging with the other without forsaking one's own beliefs.

The engagement with the other, as Aquinas practiced, also demanded of him a thorough understanding of their perspective. He immersed himself in the texts of Jewish and Islamic scholars, drawing from their wells of wisdom, not as one who seeks to plunder but as one who seeks to understand. This act of reaching across the divide was radical for its time and remains instructive for ours.

Moreover, Aquinas's life itself was a model of humility and patience, virtues requisite for any who wish to engage meaningfully with those of divergent viewpoints. His demeanor invited dialogue rather than dissent, understanding rather than umbrage. It is, therefore, no surprise that his teachings have transcended the boundaries of his time, speaking with pertinence to our present condition.

In our era, marked by division and discord, the Thomistic approach to engaging with the other offers a beacon of hope. It reminds us that at the heart of all religions and philosophies lies the pursuit of truth, a pursuit that benefits immeasurably from openness, dialogue, and mutual respect.

Aquinas's method of engagement was not merely intellectual but deeply spiritual. He approached each dialogue with prayer, seeking not victory but greater understanding. This spiritual orientation did not obscure his intellect but sharpened it, for he understood that the spirit and the mind are not competitors but co-travelers on the path to truth.

Today, as we navigate the complexities of interfaith dialogue and philosophical pluralism, Aquinas's model offers a compass. It tells us that truth is not diminished by engagement with the other but is rather deepened and enriched. His life and works encourage us to approach our dialogues with humility, respect, and a genuine desire for understanding.

The legacy of Aquinas in engaging with the other challenges us to look beyond the confines of our own convictions. It beckons us to step into the vast field of human thought with the assurance that all truth, wherever it may be found, leads ultimately to the Divine. This assurance frees us to explore, question, and ultimately grow in our faith and understanding.

In conclusion, engaging with the other, as Aquinas has shown, is not merely an intellectual exercise but a profound spiritual journey. It is a path marked by the quest for truth, guided by faith and reason. For those who dare to walk it, it promises not only greater understanding but an ever-deepening love for the Divine. Thus, may we, following in the footsteps of Aquinas, engage with the other not as adversaries but as fellow pilgrims on the journey toward truth.

Let us then, with Aquinas as our guide, embark upon this journey with open hearts and minds, ready to discover that the truth we seek, in its multifaceted beauty, is ever before us, inviting us to engage, understand, and ultimately embrace. In this endeavor, may we find not only wisdom but also the peace that comes from the assurance that all truth, being of the Divine, unites rather than divides. Thus equipped, let us go forth, engaging with the other in the spirit of Aquinas, with charity, humility, and fervent hope.

Universal Truths and Shared Values

In this age of discord and division, where the chasm 'twixt faiths seems insurmountable, the teachings of Aquinas illuminate a path to unity. Verily, within the vast tapestry of his works, lies a profound acknowledgment of universal truths and shared values that transcend the boundaries of disparate belief systems. Aquinas, with his sagacity, argued not for the supremacy of one creed over another but advocated for dialogue rooted in mutual respect and the quest for wisdom. It is this pursuit of common ground—of virtues such as justice, temperance, courage, and prudence—that serves as the bedrock for interfaith understanding. Thus, in embracing Thomism, we find not only a framework for reconciling differences but also a beacon of hope for fostering peace and goodwill amongst all peoples. Through his lens, we perceive that beneath the myriad rituals and doctrines, there pulses the heart of a shared humanity, yearning for truth, beauty, and the divine.

Building Bridges In the vast continuum of history, wherein doctrines have been both shield and spear, the labor of Thomas Aquinas standeth as a beacon of reconciliation betwixt faith and reason. With great care and dedication, this illustrious sage of yore didst embark upon a noble quest, weaving together the threads of disparate worlds into a tapestry of understanding most divine. It is upon this very fabric that our discourse now treadeth, exploring the labyrinths of belief with the luminescence of Aquinas's wisdom to guide us.

Consider, if thou wilt, the grand cathedrals of thought erected by minds unbound by the temporal. Within these sacred halls, Aquinas, like a master mason, laid the cornerstone of dialogue betwixt faiths. His was not a realm fenced by dogma, but rather an open forum, where the exchange of divine contemplations fostered unity amidst diversity. 'Tis this ethos of intellectual embrace that carved paths through mountains of misunderstanding, urging all who seek truth to journey together, irrespective of creed.

Esteemed reader, this discourse ventures now into the realm of interfaith dialogue, where many a scholar hath tread with trepidation. Yet, Aquinas, with the grace of one anointed in wisdom, navigated these tempestuous waters with a compass of philosophical and theological acumen. His discourses on the nature of the divine, the essence of being, and the moral imperative of virtue served as bridges over which the faithful of varied persuasions might traverse.

In his engagements with the works of Aristotle, a philosopher from the climes of pagan antiquity, Aquinas exemplified a magnanimity of spirit. By integrating Aristotelian philosophy into the heart of Christian theology, he demonstrated that truth, irrespective of its source, contributes to the illumination of divine understanding. This act of reconciliation 'twixt Athenian wisdom and Christian revelation, standeth as testament to the virtuous potential of interfaith dialogue.

Moreover, the Summa Theologica, Aquinas's magnum opus, serveth as a grand edifice of theological discourse, wherein the stones of Judaic, Islamic, and Ancient wisdom are found alongside those quarried from

Christian grounds. In his treatment of the laws of nature and divine governance, Aquinas drew upon the insights of Maimonides, a Jewish sage, and Averroes, an Islamic philosopher, with equal reverence and scholarly rigor.

'Twould be an oversight most grave to ponder the contributions of Aquinas to interfaith dialogue without considering his profound respect for human reason. In his view, reason and faith were not adversaries in a duel to the death, but rather companions in pursuit of truth. This respect for reason created a common ground upon which dialogue 'twixt faiths could prosper, fostering an environment where mutual understanding could flower amidst the thorns of contention.

As we navigate the complexities of modern religious discourse, the methods of Aquinas offer a beacon of hope. In a world torn asunder by strife and discord, his approach inviteth us to seek commonality in our shared pursuit of the divine. This path, though fraught with challenges, promiseth a horizon where the sun of understanding riseth to dispel the shadows of ignorance and fear.

It bears mentioning that Aquinas's endeavors in building bridges extended beyond the earthly to the celestial. His theological works endeavor to reconcile the human soul with the Divine Essence, a task of no small consequence. By arguing that the beatific vision—the ultimate union with God—is the end towards which all human life aspires, he laid a foundation for interfaith commonality in the ultimate purpose of human existence.

In discussions of moral philosophy, too, Aquinas offered gems of wisdom that might adorn the crown of any faith. His discourse on the virtues, both natural and theological, proffers a blueprint for a life well-lived, transcending the boundaries of individual religions. By championing virtues such as prudence, justice, fortitude, and temperance, he provided a moral compass universal in its appeal and application.

Yet, let us not be blinded by the brilliance of Aquinas's intellect alone. The man himself, in his humility and devotion, exemplified the very principles he espoused. His life, marked by prayer, asceticism, and an unyielding pursuit of divine truth, serves as a bridge between the realms of contemplation and action. In embodying the virtues he so ardently philosophized, Aquinas demonstrated how faith and reason, together, can elevate the human condition.

In summoning the courage to engage with the Other, Aquinas teaches us the value of intellectual humility. Admit we must, that no single tradition holdeth monopoly over truth. Rather, in the multitude of voices, in the symphony of beliefs, lieth the greater understanding we seek. Aquinas's legacy, thus, is not merely one of theological or philosophical import, but a clarion call to embrace the other with open heart and mind.

As we tread the path of dialogue and understanding, we ought to bear in mind the lessons of Aquinas. In a world fractured by divisions, his teachings illuminate a way forward, embracing diversity, nurturing dialogue, and fostering a profound respect for both faith and reason. His work, transcendent in its wisdom, inviteth us to a table of fellowship where all are welcome, and from which none depart hungry.

In conclusion, the endeavor to build bridges, as exemplified by Thomas Aquinas, is not the undertaking of a moment, but the work of ages. It requireth patience, understanding, and a ceaseless commitment to the pursuit of unity amidst diversity. Let us, inspired by the legacy of this great saint and scholar, dedicate ourselves anew to this noble task, that we might, together, forge a future marked by peace and mutual respect.

Thus, in the spirit of Aquinas, let us journey forth with minds open and hearts attuned to the divine symphony of creation. For in the endeavor to understand the Other, we embark upon the noblest of quests: the quest for truth, for understanding, and for the harmonious coexistence of all God's creation. In this, may we find the fulfillment of Aquinas's vision, and in so doing, draw ever nearer to the divine.

The Triumph of Thomistic Philosophy

Upon the foundation laid by chapters foregone, we hence find ourselves in the midst of a veritable garden of intellectual blossoming, wherein the philosophy birthed by Thomas Aquinas doth not simply survive but indeed thrives and governs the souls of those seeking enlightenment. With acute vigor, this chapter shall unfold the manner in which Thomistic thought did overcome the grievous objections laid at faith's doorstep, not through mere force of will but by the power of logical prowess and profound personal conviction. 'Tis a tale of how logic, when wielded by a master such as Aquinas, serves not as the slayer of faith but as its staunchest guardian, leading those entangled in the webs of scepticism towards the light of understanding and, ultimately, to the embrace of Jesus Christ as the sovereign truth. Herein, the victory of Thomistic philosophy is revealed not merely in the conquest of intellectual territories but in the salvation it brings to souls adrift, guiding them to safe harbor through the tempests of doubt and despair, and anchoring them in the bedrock of an enlightened faith.

Overcoming Objections to Faith

In the vibrant tapestry of Thomistic philosophy, where threads of divine contemplation intertwine with the warp and weft of human reasoning, lies the power to vanquish the shadows of doubt cast upon the sanctity of faith. Within the realm shaped by the sagacious mind of Thomas Aquinas, the scepter of truth and the blade of logic are wielded with equal finesse, cutting through the skepticism that clouds the hearts of men. For Aquinas, faith and reason exist not as adversaries locked in eternal combat but as allies, each affirming the other's worth in the quest for ultimate truth. He did champion the cause that to believe is an act not of intellectual surrender, but of embracing a higher form of wisdom, accessible yet profound. This hallowed convergence of faith and reasoning emerges as the bulwark against which objections to faith find no purchase, for in the luminance of Thomistic thought, every doubt is but a shadow that yearns for the light of understanding. Thus, the triumph of Thomistic philosophy illuminates the path for souls ensnared in the throes of disbelief, beckoning them towards the sanctity of faith, where lies the true solace for the seeking mind and the restless heart.

Logical Arguments and Personal Conviction As we traverse the intellectually rigorous landscapes crafted by the likes of Thomas Aquinas, a singular comprehension begins to take shape, melding the profound with the personal. For within the voluminous works of Aquinas, particularly his magnum opus, the Summa Theologica, lies a detailed exposition on the nature of God's existence and essence — a foundation built upon logical argumentation and deeply rooted personal conviction.

In the dialectical journey towards truth, Aquinas artfully navigates through logic and faith, intertwining them in such a manner that they cease to stand as opposing forces. He proposes, instead, a harmonious union where reason serves faith, and faith uplifts reason. This interplay, as observed in the Summa Theologica, forms a compelling discourse that extends an olive branch to those ensnared by skepticism.

Consider the Five Ways proposed by Aquinas as a testament to God's existence. Herein, the clarity of logical argumentation springs forth, each Way building upon the last, forming a sturdy lattice work of reason. Yet, underlying these arguments is a profound personal conviction in the truth of God, showcasing Aquinas's belief that logic does not detract from faith, but validates it.

The intertwining of logical arguments with personal conviction in Aquinas's discourse offers a bridge to understanding for atheists and agnostics. By presenting a rational basis for God's existence, complemented by a palpable conviction, Aquinas extends a dialogue that is both intellectually satisfying and spiritually enriching.

However, the path Aquinas treads is not solely reliant upon the apologetic might of logical discourse. For alongside the intellect's quest for understanding, there lies a heartfelt conviction born out of personal encounter and experiential knowledge of the divine. This duality forms the crucible within which Aquinas's arguments are forged, providing them with a singular vitality.

It is within the Summa's exploration of cause and effect, motion, contingency, and other metaphysical realities, that the seeker may find echoes of their own quest for truth. Aquinas's method, rooted in Aristotelian logic and Christian doctrine, does not shy away from addressing the profound questions that stir within the human spirit. His conviction illuminates his logic, making his conclusions not merely academic exercises, but testaments of faith.

To engage with Aquinas demands a willingness to venture deep into the realms of thought and belief, where logical arguments serve not as cold abstractions, but as living pathways leading towards spiritual enlightenment. In this journey, personal conviction acts as the compass guiding one through the labyrinth of reason towards the light of faith.

One encounters, in the personal conviction of Aquinas, a beacon of certainty amidst the often tumultuous seas of doubt and questioning. His unwavering faith, coupled with rigorous intellectual labor, stands as an indomitable testament to the power of belief informed by reason.

The dialogues and discourses of Aquinas, particularly those addressing the existence and nature of God, do not merely seek to convince through logic alone. They aim to transform, through a synthesis of argument and conviction, leading one towards a deeper, more profound understanding of faith.

As one delves further into the philosophical and theological territories charted by Aquinas, it becomes increasingly clear that his logical arguments are not ends in themselves, but means to a greater end — the cultivation of personal conviction in the truth of God's existence and benevolence.

For Aquinas, the intellectual endeavor of theology is an act of worship, a sanctified pursuit wherein logic and reason are wielded as instruments of faith. This perspective offers a profound insight for modernity, where often faith and reason are seen in opposition rather than as complementary facets of the human experience.

Through the lens of Aquinas, logical arguments for the existence of God become more than mere academic pursuits; they evolve into spiritual exercises, opportunities for the heart and mind to converge upon a single point of truth. Personal conviction, thus, is not blind faith but an informed choice, grounded in the rigors of rational thought and illuminated by the light of divine revelation.

In engaging with the skeptics of his time, Aquinas demonstrated an unwavering confidence in the power of reasoned discourse to reveal truth. Yet, his ultimate reliance lay in the strength of personal conviction, fostered by a deep and abiding relationship with the divine.

This synthesis of logic and belief, reason and faith, carries a timeless relevance. In an era where skepticism and faith often appear at loggerheads, the works of Aquinas offer a blueprint for dialogue, a testament to the enduring power of logical arguments informed by personal conviction.

Thus, as we look upon the intellectual legacy of Thomas Aquinas, let us not merely see a scholar of immense erudition but a seeker who journeyed through the landscapes of logic and faith with an unwavering conviction in pursuit of the divine. It is here, at the confluence of reasoned argument and heartfelt belief, that Aquinas invites us to discover the true essence of faith — a faith not blind, but illuminated by the light of reason.

The Ultimate Victory

In the final analysis, the triumph of Thomistic philosophy can be seen as nothing less than the ultimate victory of enlightenment and salvation through Jesus. Amidst a world torn asunder by doubt, where shadows of disbelief cast long upon the soul's quest for truth, Thomas Aquinas emerged as a beacon of divine wisdom. Through his profound insights, he forged an indomitable bridge 'twixt faith and reason, manifesting the luminescence of the Gospel's truth to those ensnared by scepticism. In his grand opus, where arguments are laid bare with the precision of a surgeon and the grace of a poet, Aquinas demonstrates that at the heart of all existence pulses the undeniable certainty of Christ's divinity. It is here, within the hallowed confines of his thought, that the sceptre of faith triumphs, illuminating the path towards enlightenment and salvation. What greater victory can there be than to guide a soul towards the eternal embrace of its Creator? Thus, through Thomistic philosophy, countless souls find their way, wandering no more in the desert of doubt, but stepping into the ineffable light of Truth, led by Aquinas' hand.

Enlightenment and Salvation Through Jesus As our discourse wendeth its way toward the zenith of Thomistic triumph, 'tis apt we delve into the doctrine most sublime, wherein lies the crux of Aquinas's sermons and scholarly travail: the enlightenment and salvation proffered through the grace of Jesus Christ. In this section, our discourse shall meander through the labyrinthine corridors of Thomistic philosophy and theology to uncover the luminescence of true wisdom bestowed upon humanity through the life and teachings of Christ, as interpreted by Saint Thomas Aquinas.

In the annals of history, many a scholar hath sought to marry the seemingly disparate entities of faith and reason. Yet, 'tis Aquinas who, with unparalleled finesse, brought to the fore the notion that true enlightenment of mind and spirit is found in the acknowledgment of Jesus as both Lord and savior. For Aquinas, the Light of Christ embodied not merely a beacon of moral guidance, but the very essence of divine wisdom accessible to human intellect.

Verily, in his voluminous treatises, Aquinas posited that all truth, be it revealed through the natural world or scripture, hath its provenance in God. 'Tis through the incarnation of Jesus, that God hath made the ultimate truth — salvation and divine wisdom — manifest unto mankind. In the person of Jesus, the divine and human natures conjoin, offering a pathway for humanity to partake in divine wisdom.

Consider, for instance, the profound implications of the Paschal Mystery — the passion, death, and resurrection of Jesus. Aquinas argued that through these events, Jesus not only reconciled humanity with the Father but also illuminated the path to true enlightenment: understanding our place in relation to God and creation. The salvific act of Christ opens the door to a wisdom that transcends mere human reason, offering insight into eternal truths.

To fathom the depths of Thomistic thought regarding salvation, one must grapple with his conception of grace and virtue. Grace, for Aquinas, is the divine assistance given to us for the meritorious actions leading to salvation. It is through grace that we are drawn closer to God, enlightened by His wisdom, and eventually attain salvation. In Jesus, grace finds its full expression — an unmerited gift allowing humans to participate in divine life.

Moreover, Aquinas elucidates the role of faith in enlightenment and salvation. Faith, as a theological virtue, enables belief in the truths revealed by God through Jesus. 'Tis not a blind belief but one that engages the intellect, allowing the faithful to discern divine truths hidden from unaided human reason. Faith in Jesus, therefore, becomes the first step toward enlightenment, guiding the intellect to apprehend divine mysteries.

In the hallowed doctrines of Aquinas, the love of God as expressed through Jesus emerges as the fulcrum of moral life and the ultimate end of human existence. Charity, or love for God and neighbor, perfected in Jesus's teachings, stands as the highest virtue, drawing souls toward the beatific vision — the ultimate intellectual enlightenment and communion with God in the afterlife.

Yet, let us not assume Aquinas's teachings diminish the importance of human reason. Instead, reason and faith are portrayed as harmonious — reason being a gift from God to lead us toward Him. The teachings and miracles of Jesus, while surpassing natural reason, invite a deeper intellectual inquiry, encouraging believers to seek understanding (fides quaerens intellectum).

The sacraments, as expounded by Aquinas, serve as the conduit of grace and truth from Jesus to the believer, nourishing the soul and enlightening the intellect. In the sacrament of the Eucharist, particularly, believers partake of the Body and Blood of Christ, achieving a profound communion with the divine wisdom and salvation.

Contemplation, as urged by Aquinas, becomes a pivotal practice for those yearning for enlightenment and salvation. Through contemplation of God's Word and works, especially as manifested in Jesus, the soul ascends to a closer understanding of divine truth. This spiritual exercise, grounded in love and faith, allows the believer to glimpse the eternal wisdom of God.

In the life and works of Jesus, Aquinas found the illustration par excellence of virtues — humility, charity, patience, and chastity. By emulating Christ, the faithful embark upon the path of moral perfection, guided by the light of divine wisdom toward the ultimate goal of salvation.

Aquinas's discourse on Jesus's role in human enlightenment and salvation illuminates the journey from mere intellectual assent to profound spiritual awakening. It is a testament to the belief that in knowing and loving Jesus, one embarks upon the true path of enlightenment — a journey not of isolation but of intimate union with God.

In concluding this treatise on Aquinas's notion of enlightenment and salvation through Jesus, let us ponder the import of integrating faith with reason. For in the embrace of Jesus's teachings and the following of His path, lies not only the hope of salvation but also the beacon of wisdom that leads the intellect from shadows into light.

Thus, the legacy of Aquinas, steeped in the teachings of Jesus, calls forth a renewed understanding of enlightenment — one that transcends mere human reason, anchoring the soul in the eternal love and wisdom of God. 'Tis a doctrine as relevant today as in the age of Aquinas, beckoning all who seek truth, wisdom, and salvation to look unto Jesus, the fount of all enlightenment.

The Timeless Relevance of Thomas Aquinas

In the annals of history, scarce are the names that hath dawned with such resplendence as that of Thomas Aquinas. As our journey through the wondrous life and monumental works of this paragon of theological and philosophical thought draweth to a close, one cannot help but stand in awe at the indelible imprint he hath left upon the realm of spiritual inquiry and beyond. It is through his teachings we find a bridge 'twixt faith and reason, a testament to the undying power of belief tempered by the rigor of intellectual pursuit.

The life of Aquinas, marked by trials and triumphs alike, serves as a beacon of light for those ensnared in the throes of doubt and disbelief. His humble beginnings, beset with familial discord and societal pressures, only heralded the emergence of a mind so attuned to the divine, that his ensuing journey would forever alter the course of theological discourse. In embracing his calling with unwavering conviction, Aquinas demonstrated the essence of true faith - a steadfast commitment to the path laid by our Creator.

As we traversed the scholarly path Aquinas embarked upon, from the hallowed halls of Paris and Cologne to his epoch-making encounters with Albertus Magnus, we witnessed the awakening of a mind so profound, its legacy would transcend the boundaries of time. Through his synthesis of Aristotelian philosophy with Christian doctrine, Aquinas furnished us with a framework within which the mysteries of faith could be approached with the tools of reason.

The Five Ways, Aquinas's unparalleled contribution to the discourse on the existence of God, stand as a monumental testament to the power of logical argumentation in matters of faith. By demonstrating the existence of a Prime Mover, a First Cause, through meticulous reasoning, Aquinas bridged the chasm 'twixt the observable world and the ineffable divine, inviting believers and skeptics alike to contemplate the foundations of belief.

In his choice of mendicancy, Aquinas eschewed the trappings of material wealth, embodying the virtues of poverty and devotion. His life as a friar, replete with the rigors of prayer, preaching, and community, exemplified the ideal of spiritual richness unfettered by worldly desires. This stark repudiation of materialism serves as a guiding light in an age beguiled by the lure of temporal gains.

Confronting heresies and upholding the sanctity of orthodoxy, Aquinas's battles were not merely against the misconceptions of his time but against the perennial challenge of misguidance in matters of faith. Through his defense of the true teachings of the Church, Aquinas demonstrated the paramount importance of vigilance and eloquence in the preservation of doctrinal purity.

The Summa Theologica, Aquinas's magnum opus, remains an unrivaled masterpiece of theological inquiry. Its meticulous organization, profound depth, and clear exposition of the principles of Christian faith render it an indispensable resource for theologians and laypersons alike. Beyond its immediate purpose, it stands as a symbol of the boundless potential of the human intellect when yoked to the pursuit of divine truth.

Yet, Aquinas's journey was not devoid of obstacles. Accusations of heresy, physical ailments, and the toll of his relentless scholarly endeavors bespeak the sacrifices entailed in the quest for enlightenment. These trials, however, only served to refine his character, imbuing his work with a profound sense of human frailty and divine grace.

The mystical experiences that marked the latter years of Aquinas's life, culminating in his declaration that all his writings seemed "like straw" in comparison to the glory of the divine revelation he had witnessed, underscore the transcendent nature of true knowledge. In this humbling realization lies a powerful message: that the ultimate aim of our intellectual and spiritual pursuits is to draw nearer to the ineffable mystery of God's presence.

In assessing the legacy of Aquinas, one cannot but marvel at the enduring relevance of his teachings. In a world fraught with discord and disillusionment, his life stands as a testament to the harmonious coexistence of faith and reason, guiding us through the tumult of contemporary debates and existential quandaries.

The call to revisit Aquinas in the face of modern challenges is not merely an academic exercise but a vital endeavor for those seeking to navigate the complexities of faith, ethics, and interfaith dialogue. His work offers a beacon of clarity, illuminating the path to understanding and tolerance in an increasingly polarized world.

Thomism, with its emphasis on logical argumentation and personal conviction, remains a potent antidote to the objections raised against faith. In Aquinas's triumph over skepticism, we find not only a vindication of belief but a compelling invitation to explore the depths of our own convictions with the rigor and openness that characterized his life's work.

The timeless relevance of Thomas Aquinas lies not merely in the breadth of his intellectual achievements but in the depth of his spiritual insight. In his synthesis of faith and reason, Aquinas offers a model of belief that transcends the confines of his era, reaching out across the ages to speak to the hearts and minds of seekers in every generation.

As we bid farewell to the hallowed journey through the life and legacy of Thomas Aquinas, let us carry forth the torch of his wisdom, illuminating our path with the beacon of faith informed by reason. May his enduring relevance inspire us to seek the divine with both the fervor of our hearts and the fullness of our minds, united in the quest for truth that transcends the boundaries of time.

Appendix A: Appendix

In the annals of history, there be few so illustrious and enlightened as Thomas Aquinas, a beacon of divine intellect amidst the murky waters of mortal reason. A sage whose life's journey from the cradle to the celestial embrace unfolded in an epoch fraught with turmoil and spiritual querulousness. This appendix serves not only as a chronological testament but as a lantern, guiding the curious and the devout through the milestones of a life consecrated to the divine pursuit of knowledge and faith. Herein, the reader shall find a meticulously crafted timeline, a chronicle that maps the pilgrimage of this paragon of Thomistic philosophy through the earthly realm.

Timeline of Saint Thomas Aquinas's Life

1. **1225** - In the hamlet of Roccasecca, in the kingdom then known as the Holy Roman Empire, Thomas was born unto the noble Aquino family. His birth, foretold by a hermit to his mother as bringing forth a mind that would kindle the world with divine wisdom.
2. **1230** - At the tender age of five, he was consigned to the monastery of Monte Cassino, where the young Thomas began his scholastic odyssey, his intellect already showing signs of the brilliance that was to define his earthly mission.
3. **1244** - Marking the year of a pivotal juncture in his life, Thomas chose the path of the Dominicans, a decision that led him to embrace poverty and devotion over the opulence that his noble birth afforded.
4. **1245-1252** - His academic pursuits led him to the University of Paris, and then to Cologne, where under the tutelage of Albertus Magnus, his intellect flourished, and his foundational ideas of faith and reason as harmonious companions took root.
5. **1256** - Thomas was accorded the title of Master of Theology at the University of Paris, a testament to his scholarly achievements and his profound understanding of divine laws and precepts.
6. **1259-1268** - In these years, his pen became his herald, crafting works that would endure as pillars of Catholic theology. Among them, the

Summa Contra Gentiles, a tome that sought to reconcile the divine with the rational.

7. **1268-1272** - Returning to Paris, Thomas found himself embroiled in academic and spiritual contests, defending the orthodoxy against burgeoning heretical tides, his erudition proving both shield and sword in the battle for souls.
8. **1273** - A year marked by divine revelation and personal transformation. After a mystical experience during Mass, Thomas declared his corpus of work as mere "straw", a humble admission that his scholarly endeavors paled in comparison to the vastness of God's truth.
9. **1274** - On his journey to the Council of Lyons, where he was to advocate for the unity of the Eastern and Western Churches, Thomas was called to his eternal reward. On March 7th, the world lost a luminary, but the heavens gained a saint.

Thus concludes our perusal through the life of Saint Thomas Aquinas, a sage whose legacy transcends the confines of time and place. His treatises, a bridge between mortal understanding and divine wisdom, continue to illuminate the path for those who seek enlightenment through faith. May this humble chronicle serve as a beacon to all who journey through the tempest of doubt and disbelief, guiding them to the harbor of truth that is found in the embrace of the divine.

Timeline of Saint Thomas Aquinas's Life

In the annals of time, few have left an indelible mark on the spheres of theology and philosophy as hath Saint Thomas Aquinas. Born in the lap of Lombardy, in the castle of Roccasecca, in the year of our Lord 1225, his journey from mortal man to saintly scholar would unfold across seven decades, leaving a legacy enshrined in the hearts and minds of those who seek the divine through reason and faith.

The early years of Thomas were swathed in the tapestry of a noble lineage, his family vying for his future to be cast in the mold of a Benedictine abbot. Yet, the whispers of destiny called him to a path less trodden, pledging his life to the Dominican Order in 1244, a decision that would kindle the ire of kith and kin, leading to his capture and confinement in the family hold. One year's time would pass 'fore he would again breathe the air of freedom, embarking henceforth on a scholarly quest that would lead him to Paris and Cologne.

Under the tutelage of the revered Albertus Magnus in Cologne, Thomas's intellect would flourish, his thirst for knowledge leading him to the University of Paris. Yet, the academic tranquility was not to last; the year 1256 bore witness to his defense of the mendicant orders, drawing the ire of secular academicians. Through trials and tribulations, his resolve remained unshaken, his faith in the Lord and his call to poverty unwavering.

The subsequent years saw Thomas Aquinas weaving his opus, the "Summa Theologica," a beacon of Thomistic theology, lighting the path for those adrift in the sea of doubt and heresy. Yet, the toils of his labor were not borne without cost; his health began to falter under the weight of his endeavors.

As the final chapter of his terrestrial sojourn approached, Aquinas experienced divine revelations that would lead him to declare, "All that I have written seems like straw to me." In 1274, en route to the Council of Lyon, called by Pope Gregory X, Thomas's health yielded to the burden of his labours, and on the 7th of March, he was called to his eternal rest in the Cistercian monastery of Fossanova.

The legacy of Saint Thomas Aquinas extends far beyond the mortal coil, his canonization in 1323 but a testament to his sanctity. His feasts are celebrated with piety, his teachings guiding the flock towards the light of faith and reason.

Ye scholars and theologians, ye University professors and students, let it be known that the life of Thomas Aquinas stands as a citadel of knowledge, his works a bridge spanning the chasm betwixt faith and reason. His sanctity and scholarship, a beacon of light guiding the wayward souls towards the divine truth that Jesus is God.

Let the timeline of Saint Thomas Aquinas's life be etched in the annals of history, a testament to his enduring legacy and the triumph of Thomistic philosophy. Through trials and tribulations, through heresies confronted and debates won, his life serves as a lantern illuminating the path towards enlightenment and salvation through Jesus.

In remembrance of his contributions, let us tread the path he hath laid, engaging in dialogues that bridge faiths, embracing truths universal, and building bridges where divide once dwelt. May the life of Thomas Aquinas inspire souls to seek the divine through the harmonious symphony of faith and reason.

As we reflect upon this chronicle, let us bear in mind the ultimate victory of Thomistic philosophy, an enlightenment that transcends temporal bounds, guiding the faithful towards the eternal embrace of the Almighty. In the timeless relevance of Thomas Aquinas's teachings, let hearts find solace, minds enlightenment, and souls salvation.

All things come to pass in divine accord, and so it was with Thomas Aquinas, whose life and works were a servant to faith, a testament to the power of divine grace acting through human intellect. His journey from the earthly realm to the embrace of Sainthood, a beacon for all who seek to reconcile the wisdom of the mind with the wisdom of the soul.

In closing, let the timeline of Saint Thomas Aquinas's life not merely be a chronicle of dates and deeds, but rather a narrative of faith's victory, of light over darkness, of divine wisdom transcending human folly. May it stand as an open invitation to all, believers and skeptics alike, to explore the depths of faith through the lens of reason, guided by the light of one of the greatest minds ever to grace this earthly plane.

Thus, we commend unto thee, the life of Saint Thomas Aquinas, a beacon of divine wisdom, whose legacy shall endure 'til the end of age, inspiring generations yet unborn to seek the Lord with all their heart, mind, and soul. Amen.

Glossary of Thomistic Terms

In the pursuit of enlightening minds and hearts, and guiding souls towards the light of Christ through the profound insights of Thomas Aquinas, we find ourselves amidst terminology not of our everyday discourse. Herein, I shall endeavor to unveil the essence of such terms, employed in the noble quest of Thomistic philosophy and theology, that they might illuminate the path for scholars and seekers alike.

A

- **Actus purus**: A term that likeneth unto the pure act, describing the Divine Being who is fully actualized, lacking naught in potentiality.
- **Analogia entis**: The analogy of being, revealing how creatures relate to their Creator in likeness yet differ vastly in perfection.
- **Aposteriori**: Knowledge gleaned from experience, perceiv'd through the senses, guiding us to discern the truths that lie beyond.
- **Aquinas**: Our blessed guide, Thomas Aquinas, whose wisdom unfurls the tapestry of faith and reason intertwined.

B

- **Beatific Vision**: The ultimate bliss, the direct sight and love of God, that souls in Heaven are granted, beholding Him in His majestic glory.

C

- **Causa prima**: The First Cause, from which all causation floweth, untouch'd by movement or change, the Unmoved Mover Himself.
- **Consubstantial**: Of the same substance or essence, as proclaimed in the mystery of the Trinity, three persons, one divine essence.

D

- **Dualism**: The division of body and soul, matter and spirit, often discussed in the context of human nature and divine intervention.

E

- **Esse**: To be, the act of existence, which Aquinas holds as the most profound act, distinguishing between essence and existence.
- **Eudaimonia**: A term borrowed from Aristotle, signifying the highest human good, flourishing through virtuous living.

F

- **Fides et ratio**: Faith and reason, the harmonious partnership whereupon the edifice of Thomistic thought is constructed.

I

- **Intelligible species**: The immaterial form through which the intellect apprehends the essence of things, a cornerstone in Aquinas' epistemology.

O

- **Ontology**: The study of being in its broadest reaches, exploring existence and reality as expounded in Thomistic principles.

P

- **Potentiality**: The capability of being but not yet in act, the foil to actus, upon which change and motion predicate.
- **Principium quoddam**: A certain principle, the foundational truths upon which logic and understanding are predicated.

Q

- **Quiddity**: The essence of a thing, what it is, considered in abstraction from individual qualities, yet defining its very nature.

S

- **Substance**: That which exists in itself, not in another, the subject to which accidents may adhere but itself remains undivided.
- **Syllogism**: A form of reasoning, a logical argumentation wherein from two premises a conclusion is inevitably drawn.

In these terms, one finds not merely the vocabulary of a bygone era but the keys to unlocking profound truths that transcend time. They are the tools wherewith Aquinas fashioned his monumental contribution to the understanding of God, man, and the cosmos. Let the minds willing to journey through the depths of Thomistic thought find here a compass, that they may navigate the seas of complex notions with greater ease and arrive at the shore of divine understanding.

Thus, in the study of these terms, let us embark upon a noble quest not for knowledge alone but for wisdom, that in understanding the essence of Thomistic theology, we might deepen our faith and draw ever closer to the heart of God. And in this pursuit, may we remember that knowledge serves faith, leading us ever towards the Beatific Vision promised to those who, by grace, persevere in the love of Christ.

Suggestions for Further Reading

In the quest for deeper understanding, many a scholar hath journeyed through the realms of thought that St. Thomas Aquinas once traversed. Herein, we extend unto thee a curated selection of texts, each a beacon of knowledge, guiding the curious mind towards the luminous truth that Aquinas himself did seek. Let these works not merely serve as tools, but companions, in thine own scholarly endeavors and spiritual quests.

The Summa Theologica of Thomas Aquinas, whilst formidable, stands as the cornerstone of Thomistic philosophy. This comprehensive guide to Catholic doctrine offers penetrating insights into the divine nature, ethics, human conduct, and the cosmos itself. Any who desire to know the mind of Aquinas shall start here, but be forewarned, its depths are vast and its treasures not easily won.

For those who find themselves daunted by the Summa's magnitude, Fergus Kerr's *Thomas Aquinas: A Very Short Introduction* provides a more accessible passage through Aquinas's thought. This tome breaks down complex theological concepts into digestible morsels, enabling novices and scholars alike to grasp the essence of Aquinas's teachings.

Embarking further into the heart of Thomistic thought, *Aquinas's Summa Theologica: A Reader's Guide* by Timothy McDermott acts as a seasoned guide through the labyrinthine passages of Aquinas's magnum opus. It lightens the reader's load with summaries, analyses, and theological commentary, rendering the densest of theological forests navigable.

Joseph Pieper's *The Silence of St. Thomas* presents a unique perspective on Aquinas's life and works, drawing attention to the moments of silence and contemplation that shaped his thought. This exploration delves into the spaces between words, where the spirit of Aquinas's philosophy truly dwells.

Thomas Aquinas's Quaestiones Disputatae reveals the dynamic and disputative side of his work, showing his engagement with the intellectual challenges of his day. This collection of disputed questions uncovers the method through which Aquinas refined his thoughts and arguments, offering a lively approach to his theology and philosophy.

G.K. Chesterton's *St. Thomas Aquinas: The Dumb Ox* presents the life and thought of Aquinas in a manner that is at once enlightening and entertaining. Chesterton, with his characteristic wit and insight, paints a portrait of Aquinas that is full of life, challenging common misconceptions and revealing the intellectual giant's profound humanity.

For a more critical look at Thomistic thought in the contemporary context, *Reading Aquinas* by Jeremiah Hackett offers essays from leading scholars on how Aquinas's philosophy and theology can be applied to modern philosophical debates. This work is highly recommended for those interested in the intersection of medieval and modern thought.

Those intrigued by the relationship between faith and reason will find solace in *Aquinas on God: The 'Divine Science' of the Summa Theologiae* by Rudi te Velde. This examination of Aquinas's treatment of God's nature provides a profound understanding of the underpinnings of Aquinas's theological and philosophical inquiry.

Exploring the ethical dimensions of Aquinas's thought, *Thomas Aquinas on Moral Wrongdoing* by Colleen McCluskey delves into his teachings on vice, sin, and human agency. It offers a nuanced interpretation of Aquinas's moral philosophy that is especially pertinent in grappling with contemporary moral dilemmas.

Aquinas and the Nicomachean Ethics, edited by Tobias Hoffmann, Jörn Müller, and Matthias Perkams, explores Aquinas's engagement with Aristotle's ethical writings. This collection reveals the Aristotelian roots of Thomistic ethics, providing valuable insights into Aquinas's synthesis of Christian doctrine and ancient philosophy.

Delving into the metaphysical aspects of Aquinas's work, *The Metaphysical Thought of Thomas Aquinas* by John F. Wippel serves as an exhaustive study of his metaphysical system. This tome meticulously examines the foundations of Aquinas's thought and its contributions to the Western metaphysical tradition.

In the realm of political thought, *Thomas Aquinas on Politics and Ethics* edited by Paul E. Sigmund compiles key excerpts from Aquinas's works that address the nature of law, justice, and governance. It equips readers with Aquinas's timeless wisdom on navigating the complexities of societal life.

Finally, for souls seeking the spiritual essence of Aquinas's teachings, *The Inner Life of St. Thomas Aquinas* by Jean-Pierre Torrell offers a window into his spiritual practices and personal devotion. This intimate portrayal enriches an understanding of how Aquinas's faith informed his scholarly pursuits.

Thus does this collection stand, a beacon for those who, stirred by the spirit of inquiry, seek to tread the path that Aquinas hath laid. May these tomes enlighten thy mind, kindle thy heart, and guide thy steps towards the luminous truth that Aquinas did himself pursue with such fervent devotion.